UNTOLD STORIES *of* OLD CURRITUCK DUCK CLUBS

UNTOLD STORIES *of* OLD CURRITUCK DUCK CLUBS

TRAVIS MORRIS

THE History PRESS

Published by The History Press
Charleston, SC 29403
www.historypress.net

Cover images: Pine Island Club with pintails in the yard. *Courtesy Laverne Brickhouse*; John Wood Foreman and Rodney Foreman in 1949 after a good day's hunt on Currituck Sound. *Courtesy Sophie F. Jordan*; John Wood Foreman's gas boat on a calm day in Currituck Sound changing men in a float box. *Courtesy Sophie F. Jordan*; and Eddie Wheatley, marsh guard and guide. *Courtesy Ernest Brickhouse*.

First published 2010
Second printing 2011
Third printing 2013

Manufactured in the United States

ISBN 978.1.59629.951.1

Morris, Travis.
Untold stories of old Currituck duck clubs / Travis Morris.
p. cm.
ISBN 978-1-59629-951-1
1. Duck shooting--North Carolina--Currituck Sound Region--History. 2. Hunting and fishing clubs--North Carolina--Currituck Sound Region--History. 3. Currituck County (N.C.)--Social life and customs. I. Title.

SK333.D8M6725 2010
799.2'4409756132--dc22
2010007880

Contents

Introduction

I have written three published books—*Duck Hunting on Currituck Sound: Tales from a Native Gunner* (2006), *Currituck Memories and Adventures: More Tales from a Native Gunner* (2007) and *Currituck: Ducks, Politics & Outlaw Gunners* (2008).

After the third book, I said that I wasn't going to write another book. Never say what you won't do. My grandmother told me that and it's true. So many people have asked me to write another book. I know that I'm nearing the end of life's journey, and there are so many tales that haven't been told; I decided I should write another book to save these stories for future generations.

There is no way I can cover all the hunting clubs that have been located in Currituck in the limited amount of space the publisher allows me.

In my first book, *Duck Hunting on Currituck Sound: Tales from a Native Gunner*, I pretty well covered Monkey Island, Whalehead and Piney Island Clubs.

In this book, I'm going to tell some tales that haven't been told and give a brief history of Currituck, Pine Island and Narrows Island Clubs, as well as stories from some of the guides who guided a few of the clubs' prestigious members and guests. I will also tell more tales from local guides of some of the old float box rigs.

When I was young, the man that I remember as being the most respected superintendent of a hunting club in Currituck was Mr. John Poyner of Currituck Shooting Club. He was superintendent there from 1909 until 1960.

My Daddy, Chester Morris, was an attorney in Currituck from 1926 until the mid-1940s, when he became a Superior Court judge, a position he held until his death in 1973. When he was practicing law, he represented many of the old duck clubs, including Currituck, Pine Island, Dews Island and Narrows Island. He also represented Mr. Joseph Palmer Knapp, who owned Mackey Island. I tell you this because a lot of the information I have about these clubs came from Daddy's files, which I had in my office until it burned down in 1980. Luckily, I had some of the papers from Currituck and Narrows Island Clubs at home and they were spared.

I can remember Mr. Poyner's daughter, Mary, bringing her dad up to my Daddy's office to tend to business. I remember that he had a green Plymouth at the time.

After Mr. Poyner died, the man who was the most respected superintendent of the clubs, in my opinion, was Mr. Carl P. White of Pine Island Club.

Mr. Carl and I became good friends in 1971 when I started developing some property for him and two other men in Corolla Village. He was the best manager of ducks I've ever known. I used to say he thought like a duck. I guess this came natural. He worked with ducks all his life. About 1910, his daddy, John Thomas White, was appointed superintendent of Narrows Island Club.

Mr. Carl grew up at the Narrows. When he was sixteen, one of the members from New York hired him as a guide. He later set himself up as a guide for hire during hunting season and worked at various jobs in the off season.

In 1935, he learned that Pine Island was being sold by its Boston members. He had guided for Mr. Austin D. Barney from Hartford, Connecticut. Mr. Carl called him and asked him to buy it and let him operate it. Mr. Barney bought it, and my Daddy handled the legal work. Pine Island was a labor of love for the rest of Mr. Carl's life.

Mr. Carl knew the older northern members of Currituck Club, and they had respect for him. In 1965, he convinced them to sell the oceanfront to Walter Davis. He told them it wouldn't hurt their duck hunting and that they could invest their money and get enough interest so it wouldn't cost them anything to operate the club. Mr. Carl was a wise investor in the stock market. He probably got a lot of tips from the powerful people he knew.

Walter Davis was vice-president of Occidental Petroleum. He lived in Midland, Texas, but was originally from Elizabeth City, North Carolina.

About this time, Mr. Barney, who owned Pine Island Club, died, and Pine Island was for sale. Atlantic Research was finished testing rocket fuel on the Whalehead property, and it was for sale. Kenyon Wilson from Elizabeth City, and a friend of Walter Davis, was attorney for Atlantic Research. Kenyon Wilson, Mr. Carl White and his stockbroker with Merrill Lynch, Stewart Hume, bought the Whalehead property. Their plan was for Occidental to buy Pine Island, and they would sell Occidental the Whalehead property and the oceanfront of the Currituck Club property. This would all be the property from sound to ocean from the Currituck Beach Lighthouse to the south end of what is known today as Sanderlin—except the sound front of the Currituck Club property. That would be the developed part that is known today as Currituck Club. This deal was all set to go through when something happened and the deal fell apart. I know what happened, but I'm not going into it here.

Gerald Friedman put a group together and bought the Whalehead property from Wilson, White and Hume. Friedman's group then gave Wilson, White and Hume out of the Whalehead Property what is known today as the Development of Corolla Village, and I developed it for them. Davis sold the Currituck Club property to James Johnson, and he developed what is now Ocean Sands. The Pine Island property was sold to Mr. Earl Slick, and Mr. Carl stayed there as superintendent as long as he lived. I'll go into that more later.

Mr. Carl's wife, Miss Rudie, was always at his side. They had two daughters, Audrey and Katherine. Audrey had two sons who were later superintendents of Currituck Club. Carl Ross ran the club from 1977 until 2001, and his brother Alex has been running it since 2001.

Mr. Carl died in 1975. He had been to my office, Currituck Realty, that day. He'd come up to my office a lot of days, and we'd sit and talk and solve the world's problems.

He taught me how the old clubs in Currituck were run when I started running Monkey Island Club. What I know about how the old clubs were run I owe to Mr. Carl. He knew a lot of people, and he opened doors for me that I couldn't open. I always felt like if I could get in the door I could take care of myself, but somebody has to let you in the door. The fact that I was a pallbearer at his funeral I think attests to our friendship.

Currituck Shooting Club

Currituck Shooting Club is said to be the oldest duck hunting club in America in continuous operation. A group of men from New York bought 3,100 acres of marsh and beach on the Currituck Outer Banks for $3,100 from Abraham Baum in 1854. Abraham Baum was my grandmother's granddaddy.

Currituck Shooting Club was incorporated on February 13, 1857, by the legislature of the state of North Carolina. The owners built a clubhouse in 1857. The sand had about taken the first clubhouse, so in 1879 they built a new, larger clubhouse that was in existence until it burned down on March 20, 2003, when it was struck by lightning. It was located directly across the sound from Poplar Branch Landing. When I heard it was on fire, Jo Ann (my wife) and I went to Poplar Branch Landing and watched it burn to the ground. I hated to see Currituck Club burn worse than I did Piney Island when it was struck by lightning August 23, 2003. John High and I started Piney Island Club. Don't get Piney Island Club and Pine Island Club confused. Piney Island is on the Intracoastal Waterway at Coinjock, and Pine Island is on Currituck Beach.

During the Civil War, the club members did not come to the club. However, a "committee" of Currituck citizens did visit the club. They took guns, ammunition, boats, decoys and other articles as spoils of war. The confiscated items were sold at Currituck Courthouse. On September 14,

Abraham Baum's house, 1857. *Courtesy Carl Ross.*

Currituck Shooting Club, 1935. *Courtesy Mary Poyner Glines.*

1865, five months after Appomattox, the club members met in New York to arrange for repairs to the clubhouse in anticipation of the upcoming hunting season. Until 1948, when Mr. Thurman Chatham got in, no southerners were admitted to membership in Currituck Shooting Club.

Currituck Club had twenty-one bedrooms and twenty-one members originally. Each member got a deed to the room. He had a liquor closet and a shell closet. Each member had his own decoys, and one person didn't use another person's stuff. The club furnished the boats, but each member hired his own guide, and in the old days it was a cardinal sin for one man to hire another member's guide.

About 1860, they had a row about women over there, so they banned women from the club. After the North Carolinians got into the club in the early 1950s, they had a problem with kids, so they banned kids.

I have a record of all the transfers of stock from 1878 until 1939. This was in the book that was in Daddy's files. Also in that book were records of the members, the officers, the Executive Committee and their addresses as of April 19, 1939. Also, Daddy had noted how he addressed each member. I'm including copies of this as I thought it might be of interest. Some of the names you will recognize include J.P. Morgan, Whitney, Vanderbilt, Havemeyer, Clyde (the steamship line) and so on.

I think this is a good place for me to tell you a little about what some of these people did for a living. This came from Mary Poyner Glines, Mr. John Poyner's daughter.

FREDERICK FOSTER BREWSTER, member, was vice-president of the United Illuminating Company and vice-president of the New Haven Savings Bank of New Haven, Connecticut. He was born on August 13, 1873, and educated at St. Paul's School, Concord, New Hampshire; he maintained memberships in the Quinnipiack Club and New Haven Country Club.

WILLIAM P. CLYDE, member, was an owner of the Clyde-Mallory Steamship Line of New York. He played an important role in the financing of the 1907–8 High School at Poplar Branch, and he gave even more toward the new Poplar Branch High School of 1916, giving as much as $5,000 at one time. Mr. Clyde and other members of the hunting clubs donated most of the $18,000 construction cost of the building. He later sold his membership in Currituck Shooting Club and formed a hunting club in Canada, where he and other members camped in the wilderness and hunted elk, bison and more. Willis Doxey was his guide at the Currituck Shooting Club, and obviously, William Clyde was named for him.

HARRY HALYBURTON and MAY HALYBURTON were from New London, Connecticut. Mr. Harry Halyburton served Currituck Shooting Club as engineer aboard its yacht, *CYGNET*. May Halyburton had the distinct job of obtaining current stock price information for club members. A telephone line connected the club with the weather station at Cape Henry, Virginia. This was the Coast Guard line. Mrs. Halyburton would place a call to the keeper, Mr. Newsome, at the Cape Henry Station and provide him with stock information that was being requested by the members of the club. Mr. Newsome would next place a call to the brokerage house on Wall Street in New York and obtain the information that Mrs. Halyburton had requested. Upon receipt of the information, Mr. Newsome in turn would place a call to Mrs. Halyburton at the Currituck Shooting Club, and she would dictate the prices on paper. When the information was completed, it was given to the butler, placed on a silver tray and then carried into the clubroom and given to the members.

HENRY O. HAVEMEYER, member, and club president of the Currituck Shooting Club, owned the American Sugar Refinery Corporation (Domino Sugar).

VALENTINE HICKS, member, was a descendant of Philip Livingston, signer of the Declaration of Independence.

JOHN PIERPONT MORGAN JR. was a member of Currituck Shooting Club. His father, Morgan Sr., had established a vast banking empire and formed the United States Steel Corporation by buying out the steel interests of Andrew Carnegie. J.P. Morgan Jr. continued his father's financial interest and is most notably remembered as the person who financed the reconstruction of Europe after the close of World War I. Mr. Morgan was head of the International Mercantile Marine, the American trust that controlled the White Star Line, the British steamship company that owned the *Titanic*. About ninety-eight years ago (from 2010), upon hearing the news of the foundering of the vessel some five hundred miles off the Newfoundland coast, Mr. Morgan arrived at the White Star Line offices in New York and waited and mingled all day with others, hoping to receive telegraphs bearing news of survivors. Mr. John Thayer, club member, lost his life in this horrible maritime disaster.

Mr. Morgan received an AB degree from Harvard in 1889. He was head of J.P. Morgan and Company in New York and Morgan Grenfell & Co., Ltd., in London. He was a trustee of the Metropolitan Museum of Art; vice-president of the New York Public Library; vice-president of the American Museum of Natural History; trustee of the Cooper Union, New York; governor of the Peabody Donation fund, London; Honorable Freeman of the Goldsmiths Company (1919); commander of the Legion of Honor; grand officer of the Order of Leopold of Belgium; grand officer of the Order of the Crown of Italy; a member of the Order of the Sacred Treasure of Japan; and received a Grand Cross of the Order of St. Gregory the Great. Mr. Morgan maintained residences at Wall Hall, Hertfordshire, England; Matinecock Point, Glen Cove, Long Island; and the Currituck Shooting Club; his other memberships included those at Athanaeum, Garrick, Whites, City of London, Roxburgh; Metropolitan; Union; New York Yacht; University; Century; Racquet (New York); Metropolitan (Washington); and Somerset (Boston).

W.K. Vanderbilt, member, continued his family's legacy of empire building. He and his wife, Alvah (who were later divorced), were social leaders in New York and Newport, Rhode Island. His son, William K. Vanderbilt Jr., was also a member of the Currituck Shooting Club. Club member William Seward Webb was married to Mr. Vanderbilt's daughter. It is obvious that John Carlo Parker, assistant to John W. Poyner, named his son, Seward Webb Parker, for Mr. Webb.

Lawrence B. Van Ingen, member after 1930, was married to an oil company heiress. Together they built and owned the Pennsylvania Turnpike.

Many of the members had private railroad cars; those who didn't went to Norfolk by train and then took the "Scooter" to Mundon's Point. The *CYGNET* would be there to take them to the club. *Courtesy Archie Johnson and Bud Coppedge.*

CYGNET, Currituck Club yacht, used to pick up members and take them to the club. *Courtesy Carl Ross.*

Gas boats at the dock at Currituck Shooting Club in the 1940s. *Courtesy Frederick C. Havemeyer II.*

Here are some recollections from Mary Poyner Glines:

> *Before adequate highways were developed, a number of the members would come for duck hunting season. This would last from November after the election until February 1st. They would arrive by private railway car at*

Munden's Point. There they would be met by their yacht, the CYGNET *and then ferried to the club where they would spend three to five days or more hunting. From Currituck some would go to Aiken, South Carolina for Quail hunting and later still on to England for grouse.*

Traveling with the members were the gentlemen's gentlemen. On the first and second floor of the club were 21 bedrooms, one for each member and furnished by that member to his personal taste. Their valets had accommodations on the third floor.

A man I knew as Uncle Ben Dobey traveled to the club from Shinnecock Hills Country Club where he worked most of the year and then he came to the Currituck Club for the hunting season then on to Aiken, South Carolina. He was in charge of preparing meals and supervising the servants for several years in the early 1900s.

A member, Mr. W.K. Vanderbilt, with several other individuals started Shinnecock Hills Golf Club in the Hamptons, on Long Island. This was the first golf club in the United States to have a clubhouse.

The members, perhaps because of their intense desire for privacy wanted this to be the most serene of retreats. They promoted a sense of decorum which was embraced not only by the members but also by everyone who had an association with the club. For example, the clubroom and dining room where the members took dinner, played cards, and relaxed at their leisure was treated with a certain reverence. Neither myself, my brothers, family relatives, or even close friends were allowed access even in the off season. This was off limits. I know this will seem a bit odd but it was as if the members were always present and this was their exclusive domain. I doubt if any of them personally felt this way, but we certainly did.

On a bulletin board was posted a regulation that religion or politics were not to be discussed among members.

All guests had to be approved in advance by the executive committee usually the President and Secretary and two other members. Then a room for the guest had to be approved by the member whose room would be used.

The members seemed to perceive there to be certain quaintness, rustic nature, a traditional quality, a place in time since passed that they wished to preserve. At the Currituck Club they would make time stand still.

There were occasions when my mother or father would propose improvements or upgrades to members' rooms or other club facilities, things which they thought would be more convenient or add to the members comfort.

These suggestions were usually met with the simple response, "We like it the way it is." Even electricity, a Delco Plant, was installed with some

> *reluctance. A door that my mother felt should be refinished to remove an annoying squeak was not to be altered lest it lose its character.*

Also from Mary Poyner Glines:

> *Superintendents of the Currituck Shooting Club*

B.F. Taylor	*February 1867–March 1872*
Thomas J. Poyner	*February 1872–April 1902*
John Calvin Gallop	*May 1902–February 1909*
John W. Poyner	*March 1909–1960*
Murray J. Chappell	*1960–1977*
Carl Ross	*1977–2001*
Alex Ross	*2001–present*

The following section is quoted from an article written for the *Winston-Salem Journal and Sentinel* and published on Sunday, December 5, 1954, by Chester S. Davis:

> *The members' room is something that should cause the eyes of a museum curator to sparkle. Those rooms…21…of them line the second floor hall above the clubroom and below the third floor dormitories of the "gentlemen's gentlemen." Each member's room is distinctive, but all share certain furnishings in common.*
>
> *The chamber pot, for example, is a collector's item fashioned of finest china and designed in a manner best described as functional. The wash basin on the stand beside the wrought-iron bed is of matching design and antiquity.*
>
> *To heat water for that basin the club member need only fire up the trim little wood stove in the corner and bring the brass kettle to a boil.*
>
> *All this is in keeping with the club's sensible attitude that if it was good enough for J.P. Morgan (as, indeed it once was) then it's quite good enough for us.*
>
> *It is the same with the skiff and decoys. Some of the hand-carved decoys date back to a time when men spoke of "gaggles of geese," "wisp of snipe," "fall of woodcock" and a "whiteness of swan."*
>
> *The furnishings in the clubroom are inclined to be a little trifle plushy. But a fringed easy chair of purple velvet blends nicely with the eagles (bald and golden) that hang from the ceiling and the enormous white swan that springs with outspread wings from one corner.*

At the far end of the clubroom there is a great glass case crammed with single specimens of all species of duck, geese, brant, swan, coot, and shore birds that have fallen before members' guns in years past.

The Old, Leisurely Days

When the Northern hunters first came into the area, the natives, who favored muzzle-loading flintlocks, were astonished at the slick English breech loaders…Prudy's, and Greener's…and the skill of the "sports" in crumpling duck high in the air.

Those were the leisurely days. The members came for weeks at a time. During the evening, while the gunners sat down to a feast of Hunger Creek oysters, roast teal, and rich red wine, the guides loaded brass shells with DuPont black powder and soft lead shot.

In the morning the members bolted their breakfast and rushed for the blinds. In those days the blinds were baited with corn, and prime shooting was assured.

The hunters sometimes shot from batteries in the open water. In those rafts with a sunken box in the center the shooters lay flat on their backs in the midst of hundreds of decoys…both wooded and live.

More often they shot from blinds on the points of marsh, from pond blinds and from pits dug in the ocean beach near places favored by the flights of geese.

Always they shot in a manner that to this day and age seems beyond belief. John Poyner likes to flip the pages of the great, red leather-bound book that contains the day-to-day shooting record of the members.

"See here," he says and points to a notation that reads, "Nov., 1885, Lewis Clark killed 444 fowl." The breakdown of that was 144 widgeon, one red head, 46 black ducks, 65 mallard, 90 geese, 11 teal, 64 gadwell, and two "sundry."

That same month David King accounted for 412 ducks and geese. Two years later…on Nov. 10, 1887 seven members spent a day on the ponds and came in with 588 ducks.

Huge Bags Ruled Out

In 1909 when John Poyner became the club's fourth superintendent, bags like that were fast becoming a thing of the past. But, he says "I recall when William D. Clyde (Clyde Steamship Lines) shot 196 geese in a single day.

And even after we had a daily limit of 100 ducks for each gun I remember a day when seven members came in with 700 ducks."

In context of today...with a limit of four ducks and two geese...that sort of slaughter is shocking. But remember, these men shot at a time when the market hunter was accepted...even admired...for his kills. Ducks, geese and swan were taken in any number and by any means, and men doubted if shooting pressure would ever damage the vast flights of waterfowl. But it did.

Automatic guns came in during the 1880s. Fast loading paper shells replaced the old brass hulls. Powder was improved and so was transportation. More and more hunters came to the marshes. And there were fewer and fewer marshes to visit.

By the turn of the century this nation was draining its wet lands to gain more acreage for the plow to scratch. Both Canada and the United States the home of the fowl was being destroyed.

The private shooting clubs were the first to appreciate the need for conservation. Like the Currituck Shooting Club, they were the first to adopt bag limits. They were also the first to ban spring shooting, limit the use of automatic guns, observe rest days, and set aside areas for fowl.

By 1905 many states had put an end to spring shooting. In 1911 New York adopted the Bayne law and prohibited the sale of game in the markets. (Although Baltimore and Washington continued to buy game the market kill fell off at Currituck as much as 50 per cent as other states followed New York's lead.)

In 1918 migratory waterfowl were put under federal regulation. The United States and Canada (later Mexico joined) began a program of international control. Spring hunting and marketing of game was outlawed all over the nation.

"Here at the club," Mr. Poyner says, "the members spent many an evening talking about ways to conserve the fowl. Some of the members were active in the fight to get guard locks put in the Albemarle and Chesapeake canal to control the polluted salt water that was coming down into Currituck Sound from Norfolk. That salt water might near destroyed our game."

FURTHER CONSERVATION

The worst came in the 1930s when drought, aggravating the harm done by over-shooting and over draining, reduced the waterfowl population to an estimated 34 million birds.

To meet that threat the bag limits were cut sharply and shooting season was shortened. The baiting of blinds, shooting over live decoys and gunning from batteries was prohibited.

"The game came back," John Poyner says. He waves his hand out over the small bay beside the club's dock. There you see the blackness of stately swans. "The fowl know who their friends are," he adds.

The blinds of Currituck Shooting club are shot from lightly. If a party hunts Canvasback Pond today, that pond will be rested for several days.

Even if the 10 members all appeared with guest during each season, the shooting still would be light. But some of them do not come at all. Henry O. Havemeyer, president of the club and the oldest member, last shot at Currituck at the time the Japanese struck at Pearl Harbor. Yet even after 15 years, his membership means much to him.

So this property is, in fact, actually a rest area for the fowl; a refuge in the heart of the duck's wintering ground that is maintained at private expense.

As a younger man, John Poyner was a hunter. "I have shot at 54 deer in my time," he says, "and I brought 53 deer out of the woods. That 54th deer? Well we found him three or four days later…lying dead in a swamp."

Part of the clubroom at Currituck Club. *Courtesy Fred Dunstan.*

The other end of the clubroom at Currituck Club. *Courtesy Fred Dunstan.*

The dining room at Currituck Club. *Left to right*: Fred Dunstan, Victor Barringer, Harry Gouas, Wooton "Dog" Lamb, Allen Ives and Bill Blount. *Courtesy Fred Dunstan.*

The Currituck Shooting Club (in the background), 1998. Kneeling are Fred Dunstan and "Dog" Lamb. *Left to right, back row*: Harry Gouas, Bill Blount, Allen Ives and Victor Barringer. *Courtesy Fred Dunstan.*

Marsh guard camp at Fosters Lead on Currituck Club property. I took this picture the day I took Francis Golden around to take pictures of some of the old clubhouses so he could paint them for *Sports Afield* magazine. Those paintings appeared in the December 1978 issue of *Sports Afield*. *Author's collection.*

He likes to tell of the great shots he has made and seen made, like the time he dropped a 19 pound swan from the air with 150 yard pistol shot.

But today with the wisdom and infirmities of age taking his eyes off the gun barrel and sending them seeking out over the marsh, John Poyner is a conservationist.

"I hear it said," he explains, "that there are men who plan to introduce in the next legislature to have the state buy this property and set it aside as a rest area for fowl."

"By jings, that's plain foolish. This is a rest area right now. We plan to keep it that way." (John and his four marsh guards keep trespassing shooters off the property. When a gunner slips by the guards, he invariably is caught, warned and sent on his way. "In 46 years I have yet to take a man to court for trespassing," Mr. Poyner says.)

Record of Transfer of Shares of Currituck Shooting Club from Date of Incorporation to July 1, 1930

DEED NO. 1				ROOM NO.
John F. Metcalf	October	1, 1878	No. 1 to	9
Henry A. Gilderslive	October	14, 1878	No. 19 to	9
Chas. R. Christy	October	9, 1880	No. 36 to	9
David King, Jr.	January	29, 1881	No. 37 to	9
Henry A. Carey	October	8, 1889	No. 63 to	9
James L. Breese	March	18, 1897	No. 72 to	9
C. L. Blair	October	30, 1911	No. 90 to	9
Percy Chubb	December	12, 1911	No. 91	9

DEED NO. 2				ROOM NO.
John F. Metcalf	October	1, 1878	No. 2 to	10
James G. Averill	October	2, 1878	No. 14 to	10
James J. Hill	July	20, 1885	No. 56 to	10
James N. Hill	March	26, 1901	No. 75 to	10
Thos. Newbold	December	23, 1902	No. 77 to	10
E. Gerry Chadwick	July	19, 1922	No. 115 to	10
George Whitney	June	17, 1929	No. 124	10

DEED NO. 3				ROOM NO.
John F. Metcalf	October	1, 1878	No. 3 to	23
Samuel Thorne	October	2, 1878	No. 15 to	23
Wm. C. Whitney	May	24, 1880	No. 34	23
Bayard Thayer	November	3, 1883	No. 19 to	23
Nathaniel Thayer	December	31, 1919	No. 110 to	23
J. Watson Webb	December	12, 1927	No. 122	23

DEED NO. 4				ROOM NO.
John F. Metcalf	October	1, 1878	No. 4 to	16
John C. Barron	October	2, 1878	No. 16	16
Wm. Woodward	October	6, 1914	No. 98	16

19

This and next two pages: Record of Transfer of Shares at Currituck Club. *Author's collection.*

DEED No. 5				ROOM NO.
Louis D. Hoard	October	1, 1878	No. 5 to	13
E. Harrison Sanford	October	20, 1879	No. 31 to	13
David King, Jr.	June	3, 1881	No. 41 to	13
Thos. H. Barber	May	2, 1882	No. 47 to	13
Samuel Russell	May	20, 1895	No. 71 to	13
Frederic N. Watriss	August	19, 1926	No. 118	13

DEED No. 6				ROOM NO.
John H. Dimon	October	1, 1878	No. 6 to	18
Louis Edwards	March	1, 1881	No. 38 to	18
Louis Edwards	May	1, 1884	No. 52 to	18
John C. Barron	April	16, 1887	No. 59 to	18
W. S. Webb	April	8, 1891	No. 66 to	18
J. H. Purdy	December	29, 1893	No. 68 to	18
F. L. Ames	June	1, 1914	No. 97 to	18
Elliot C. Bacon	May	26, 1922	No. 114 to	18
Oliver Iselin	December	1, 1924	No. 125	18

DEED No. 7				ROOM NO.
James G. Averill	October	1, 1878	No. 7 to	7
George C. Clark	December	31, 1888	No. 61 to	7
W. Seward Webb	June	17, 1889	No. 62 to	7
C. L. Blair	December	10, 1917	No. 102 to	7
J. P. Morgan	December	21, 1917	No. 104 to	7
Geo. F. Baker, Jr.	April	28, 1921	No. 111 to	7
Henry W. Bull	November	7, 1927	No. 120	7

DEED No. 8				ROOM NO.
Newton Dexter	October	1, 1878	No. 8 to	20
Wm. L. Beckwith	December	20, 1878	No. 22 to	20
Lewis Edwards	January	4, 1879	No. 23 to	20
Dr. John C. Barron	May	12, 1885	No. 55 to	20
Bayard Thayer	November	16, 1885	No. 57 to	20
John Eliot Thayer	February	5, 1903	No. 79 to	20
Wm. B. Duncan	November	23, 1927	No. 121 to	20
Lewis Cass Ledyard, Jr.	June	6, 1930	No. 126 to	20

21

DEED No. 9				ROOM NO.
Wm. L. Beckwith	October	1, 1878	No. 9 to	19
F. Augustus Schermerhorn	February	5, 1891	No. 65 to	19
Arthur Iselin	November	10, 1919	No. 108	19

DEED No. 10				ROOM NO.
Wilkins U. Hidden	October	1, 1878	No. 10 to	14
Wm. P. Clyde, Jr.	December	9, 1918	No. 100 to	14
James A. Stillman	November	14, 1919	No. 109	14

DEED No. 11				ROOM NO.
Geo. B. Post	October	1, 1878	No. 11 to	22
Geo. Von L. Meyer	September	7, 1914	No. 99 to	22
Richard Simpkins	October	30, 1919	No. 106	22

DEED No. 12				ROOM NO.
Dr. John F. Metcalf	October	1, 1878	No. 12 to	1
Louis Edwards	October	2, 1878	No. 17 to	1
Wm. C. Whitney	May	24, 1880	No. 35 to	1
Geo. C. Clark	May	10, 1881	No. 40 to	1
J. Louis Webb	November	6, 1890	No. 64 to	1
Arthur O. Choate	December	6, 1927	No. 123	1

DEED No. 13				ROOM NO.
Henry Metcalf	October	1, 1878	No. 13 to	17
David King, Jr.	May	24, 1880	No. 33 to	17
W. K. Vanderbilt	November	14, 1894	No. 70 to	17
W. K. Vanderbilt, Jr.	January	27, 1903	No. 78 to	17
Henry O. Havemeyer, Jr.	May	6, 1908	No. 88 to	17
Horace Havemeyer	July	31, 1908	No. 89 to	17
John B. Dennis	October	1, 1912	No. 92 to	17
C. Ledyard Blair	October	23, 1913	No. 95 to	17
Frederick Brewster	November	24, 1913	No. 96	17

DEED No. 14				ROOM NO.
Chas. H. Senff	October	14, 1878	No. 18 to	21
Henry O. Havemeyer, Jr.	March	21, 1906	No. 85	21

23

DEED No. 15				ROOM NO.
Wm. R. Garrison	October	25, 1878	No. 20 to	8
John F. Metcalf	October	26, 1878	No. 21 to	8
Thos. H. Barbour, U.S.A.	October	31, 1879	No. 32 to	8
George Bird	February	3, 1887	No. 58 to	8
C. Ledyard Blair	November	10, 1912	No. 93 to	8
Chas. M. Chapin	October	23, 1913	No. 94	8

DEED No. 16				ROOM NO.
Thos. J. Havemeyer	April	1, 1879	No. 24 to	5
H. O. Havemeyer, Sr.	March	16, 1882	No. 44 to	5
George C. Clark	December	21, 1883	No. 50 to	5
James J. Hill	December	2, 1884	No. 53 to	5
George S. Brewster	February	2, 1905	No. 83 to	5
John H. Prentice	October	6, 1919	No. 105 to	5
Reginald Fincke	December	4, 1925	No. 117	5

DEED No. 17				ROOM NO.
J. O. Donner	April	1, 1879	No. 25 to	6
Chas. J. Havemeyer	May	12, 1879	No. 27 to	6
H. O. Havemeyer, Sr.	March	16, 1882	No. 45 to	6
George C. Clark	December	21, 1883	No. 51 to	6
James J. Hill	December	2, 1884	No. 54 to	6
Oliver G. Jennings	February	2, 1905	No. 82	6

DEED No. 18				ROOM NO.
Wm. H. Furman	April	1, 1879	No. 26 to	2
Thos. J. Havemeyer	May	12, 1879	No. 28 to	2
Geo. B. Post	November	10, 1881	No. 42 to	2
Chas. A. Post	November	16, 1881	No. 43 to	2
Wm. K. Post	December	29, 1893	No. 67 to	2
Geo. B. Post	January	12, 1901	No. 74 to	2
John Magee	December	4, 1905	No. 84 to	2
J. Insley Blair	June	21, 1907	No. 86 to	2
C. L. Blair	December	4, 1917	No. 101 to	2
J. Sanford Barnes	December	18, 1917	No. 103	2

25

DEED No. 19				ROOM NO.
Dr. John F. Metcalf	June	27, 1879	No. 29 to	12
Geo. C. Clark	August	14, 1882	No. 48 to	12
James J. Hill	April	18, 1887	No. 60 to	12
Louis W. Hill	March	26, 1901	No. 76 to	12
C. Ledyard Blair	October	27, 1904	No. 80 to	12
Goodhue Livingston	December	23, 1904	No. 81	12

DEED No. 20				ROOM NO.
H. O. Havemeyer, Sr.	October	13, 1879	No. 30 to	15
Louis C. Clark	May	10, 1881	No. 39 to	15
Archibald Rogers	November	14, 1894	No. 69 to	15
Wm. P. Clyde	August	6, 1907	No. 87 to	15
S. B. P. Trowbridge	October	30, 1919	No. 107 to	15
Louis C. Clark, Jr.	March	9, 1925	No. 116	15

DEED No. 21				ROOM NO.
H. O. Havemeyer, Sr.	March	16, 1882	No. 46 to	11
C. L. Blair	January	12, 1901	No. 73 to	11*
C. L. Blair	September	5, 1921	No. 112 to	11
Reginald Brooks	December	27, 1921	No. 113 to	11
Geo. C. Clark	October	1, 1927	No. 119	11

*Cancelled in error; No. 112 issued instead.

CURRITUCK SHOOTING CLUB AS OF 4/19/39
POPLAR BRANCH, NORTH CAROLINA.
OFFICERS

17 members
4 estates
21 shares

Pres.	Henry O. Havemeyer, 111 B'way., Suite 1416, N.Y.C.
Vice-Pres.	- - -
Secty. & Treas.	Arthur Iselin, 357 Fourth Ave., N.Y.C.
Supt.	John W. Poyner, Poplar Branch, N.C.

EXECUTIVE COMMITTEE

J. Watson Webb, Chairman	99 John St., N.Y.C.
Col. Arthur H. Carter	c/o Haskins & Sells, 15 Broad St. NYC.
Harold T. White	c/o White, Weld & Co., 40 Wall St. "

Officers and record of members as of April 19, 1939. *Author's collection.*

MEMBERS

		Address Them
sh. Brewster, Frederick F.	129 Church St. New Haven, Conn.	Dear Mr. Brewster
1 sh. Brewster, Frederick	c/o Paine, Webber & Co., Rand Tower, Marquette Ave. & 6th St., Minneapolis, Minn.	"
1 sh. Bostwick, Dunbar W.	99 John St., NYC.	Dear Mr. Bostwick,
1 sh. Carter, Col. Arthur H.	c/o Haskins & Sells, 67 Broad St., NYC.	Dear Colonel Carte
1 sh. Dillon, Herbert L.	15 Broad St.,	Dear "Herb"
1 sh. Henry O. Havemeyer	111 B'way., N.Y.C.	
1 sh. Iselin, Arthur	357 4th Ave., N.Y.C.	Dear Arthur
1 sh. Iselin, Oliver	90 Worth St., N.Y.C.	Dear "Ollie"
1 sh. Mitchell, Cornelius von E.	350 Madison Ave. NYC.	Dear Mr. Mitchell
1 sh. Stillman, James A.	906 Park Ave., NYC.	Dear "Jim"
1 sh. Van Ingen, Lawrence B.	c/o Racquet & Tennis Club, 370 Park Ave	Dear Mr. Van Ingen
1 sh. Webb, J. Watson.	99 John St., NYC.	Dear Watson
1 sh. Webb, Samuel B.	99 John St. N.Y.C.	Dear Mr. Webb
1 sh. Webb Vanderbilt	61 Broadway, N.Y.C.	Dear Mr. Webb.
1 sh. White Harold T.	C/O White, Weld & Co. 40 Wall St. N.Y.C.	Dear Mr. White
1 sh. Whitney George	23 Wall St. N.Y.C.	Dear George
1 sh. Woodward William	1 Wall St. N.Y.C.	Dear "Bill"

(over)

Note the way Daddy addressed them.

Notes on how Daddy addressed the individual members in letters. *Author's collection.*

In later years, duck hunting got bad, the members fell off and they were having trouble getting new members. Mr. Thurman Chatham was a congressman from North Carolina who owned Dews Island. He also owned Chatham Blanket Company in Elkin, North Carolina. His brother-in-law, Jim Hanes, was president of Hanes Hosiery Company, and he was a member of a salmon fishing club in Canada.

He invited Mr. Chatham to go salmon fishing with him there in June 1948. A member of Currituck Club was also a member of that club, and he and Mr. Chatham got to talking. The man was telling Mr. Chatham about the hard time they were having getting members. Mr. Chatham agreed to buy two shares in Currituck Club for $1,000 per share. John said they didn't really put a value on the land until they sold the oceanfront to Walter Davis. They just looked at it as marsh and sand. Of course, he had to be voted on before he could actually become a member.

John Wright Jr. was superintendent of Dews Island Club for Mr. Chatham. In December 1948, John Jr. and Mr. Chatham spent one night at Currituck Club. They were invited as guests. John told me as far as he knew that this was

Chester Ralph Morris, my father. It is because Daddy represented the Currituck Shooting Club while practicing law in Currituck from 1926 until he became a Superior Court judge in 1944—a position he held until he died in 1972—that I'm able to give you the foregoing records of the members. This picture is of a portrait presented to Currituck County that now hangs in the judge's chambers of the new Currituck County Courthouse. *Author's collection.*

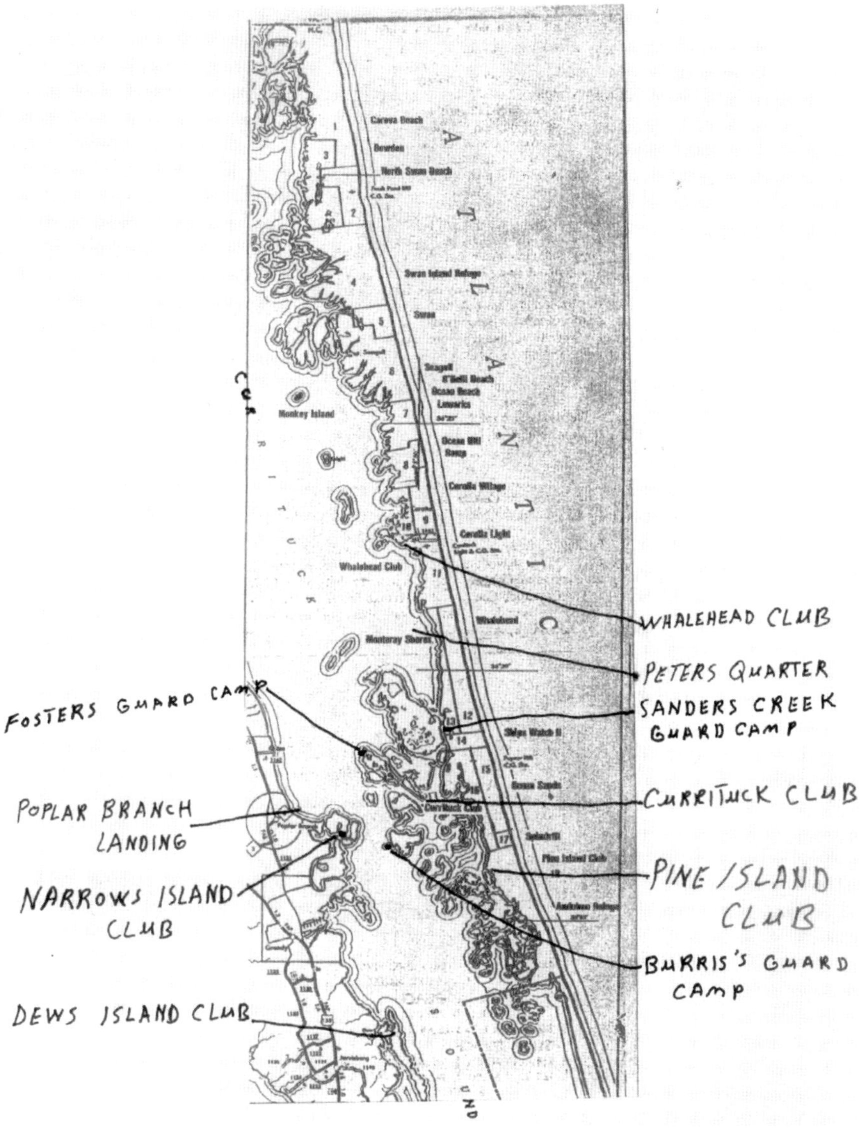

Map showing clubhouses, guard camps and Poplar Branch Landing. *Detail of DOT map from Currituck County.*

the only night Mr. Chatham ever spent there. He would stay at Dews Island, and they would go to Currituck Club in the boat to hunt. Mr. Chatham liked to talk to people, and there weren't usually many people at Currituck Club. In January 1949, Mr. Chatham was voted in, and this was the first time they had ever allowed a member to own more than one share.

Dr. Hall, *left*, and Murray Chappell, fifth superintendent of Currituck Shooting Club. *Courtesy Levie Bunch Jr.*

It had gotten down in the early to late 1940s when they may have two or three parties the whole season. John said along then that there was hardly ever over eight guns hunting a day.

John told me the old members that he knew were the old really blue-blooded Yankees and were really nice people. He said they were almost a breed of people in themselves. Some that John remembered were Mr. Mitchell, Mr. Payne (Payne-Weber) and Mr. Prescott, who wore a Scottish shooting suit with red and black leggings and a plaid cap.

The previous information from the time Mr. Thurman Chatham got in the club to this point came from a taped conversation I had with John Wright Jr. in the 1970s.

Working at Currituck Shooting Club in 1960 and 1961

As Told by Newton Hampton

Mr. John Poyner was the fourth superintendent of Currituck Shooting Club. He was there from 1908 until he retired in 1960.

Mr. Murray Chappell resigned his job as agriculture teacher and basketball coach at Dr. W.T. Griggs School (formerly Poplar Branch High School), a job he held from 1938 until he resigned in 1959. He resigned to take Mr. John Poyner's place as superintendent of Currituck Shooting Club, hereafter referred to as Currituck Club.

When Mr. Chappell first went to Currituck Club, there were no bathrooms in the clubhouse. There was a walkway between the clubhouse and the guides' quarters that had a roof over it. Off this walkway was a privy with several stalls. Each stall had a seat with a hole in it and a copper pan under it. This pan could be pulled out from the back on the outside. The houseman or janitor had to empty this every day.

When Mr. Chappell went there, he put in bathrooms and modernized the kitchen. When time came for hunting season, he called Newton Hampton and Nickolas Newbern to see if they wanted to guide there. They both took the jobs. They would be paid a weekly salary and stay at the club from Sunday afternoon until Saturday afternoon. You could come back Sunday afternoon or early Monday morning. Newton said he always came back Sunday afternoon because he didn't want to get up that early Monday morning. Cecil Brickhouse was already working there "year 'round kinda" as Mr. Chappell's assistant.

Newton Hampton and Graham Keaton at Currituck Sports in December 2009. Newton and Graham didn't have a picture of themselves when they were guiding at Currituck Club. Several of us gather at Currituck Sports every morning. I decided that this was the best place to get their picture. Ed O'Neal, who owns the store with his wife, Sybil, gets there a little before 5:00 a.m.; next is Ralph Berry, followed by the oldest member of the group, Marshall Kight, who is in his eighties; following is Newton Hampton, myself and Graham Keaton. Newton, Graham and I get there at 6:30 a.m. or a little before. We solve the world's problems. At exactly 7:00 a.m., Marshall gets up and shuffles out. His wife, "Priss," has his breakfast ready, and if he's five minutes late she gets afraid something has happened to him, and she'll be calling Ed. Newton has to go carry the mail, I go to the office and I guess Graham and Ralph Berry go home; they leave at the same time anyway. They are retired. *Author's collection.*

Mr. Chappell took all the decoys and skiffs, went through them and fixed up two good rigs. They each had an outboard motor. Up until that time, they didn't allow outboard motors in the ponds; you had to pole. They wouldn't allow the guides to carry a gun. You had to knock the cripples in the head with a shoving pole. They finally got that changed. They told Mr. Chappell they were just losing too many ducks, so he talked the members into changing that rule so the guides could carry guns.

The club only allowed double barrel, or over-and-unders. The guides had automatics. They were allowed to take them but could only put one shell in at a time.

In the summer, Mr. Chappell and Cecil Brickhouse had rebuilt the dykes to hold the water in the ponds when the tide was low. They also rebuilt the ramps with rollers they used to pull the skiff over the dyke. It had a walkway with railings there, too. You pulled the skiff up beside the dyking, and the sportsman would get out onto the walkway; then you would pull the skiff up on the rollers and get it over in the pond. The sportsman would get back in, and you went to the blind.

Some of the men would help you pull the skiff over and some wouldn't. The younger ones would help you. The older men, who were used to coming like it had been and used to being waited on, wouldn't help you.

One of the members who came was Mr. Payne from New York. He was the Payne in the stock brokerage firm of Aver, Procter and Payne.

One day, Newton had Mr. Richardson out there in Little Wills Island pond. That is the most northern pond on the Currituck Club property. It was freezing cold and the tide was high. Water was all over the marsh. They always put the sportsmen in the blind before they tied the decoys out. The guide didn't stay in the blind; he stayed in the skiff in the boat hide, which was close to the blind. He had to watch for the ducks and say "Mark right," "Mark left" or "Mark center."

He got Mr. Richardson up on the walkway, opened the blind door for him and backed up on the walkway a little to let him by. When he passed Newton with both arms full, his elbow hit Newton just hard enough to knock him off balance. He was swinging his arms trying to regain his balance when he lost it, and in a split second he was flat on his back in the water in the marsh. Newton said he could still feel that water coming in all the cracks of his clothes.

He scrambled around and got back up on the walkway. By that time, Mr. Richardson was in the blind. Newton said, "I looked at him and he looked at me, and I said, 'Are you going to the house with me or you going to stay?' He said, 'I'll stay. Throw me a couple of decoys out here when you go by the front of the blind. I'll be here when you get back.'"

Newton went on out of the pond. The Fosters Lead Guardhouse was not far, so he went there. Both marsh guards were there, Mr. Mark Aydlett and Mr. Hill Mercer. Cecil Brickhouse was also there with the gas boat. Brickhouse had dropped Newton and Mr. Richardson off in the morning and then gone to the guard camp.

Newton tied up to the dock there and said he was just a sheet of ice. He told Cecil what had happened, and Cecil said he'd take the skiff and go back and stay with the man. Cecil said, "You stay here until lunch and then come pick me up with the gas boat."

When Newton walked in the door of the camp, Mr. Aydlett and Mr. Mercer said, "My God Amighty boy, what has happened to you?" He said,

"I fell overboard" and told them what had happened. They had plenty of wood and a tin heater going in there. They threw more wood in the stove, opened the draft and in a few seconds it was cherry red. He took every stitch of clothes he had on off and hanged them up around the stove, and by lunch they were dry enough to put back on. He took the gas boat and went and picked up Cecil and Mr. Richardson.

About twenty-five years later, Newton and his daughter, Lisa, were delivering a load of corn to Currituck Club. Alex Ross was superintendent then, and Newton asked him if anybody was down hunting. He said, "Yes, there is a Mr. Richardson down here." Newton said, "It can't be." Then Alex said it was his son. Newton said he had carried Mr. Richardson and his son when his son was just a little boy. He asked how long before they'd be coming in. Alex said it shouldn't be long, as he was looking for them anytime. Newton said he'd wait, and it wasn't long before they saw a skiff coming. He walked down to the dock and introduced himself. Ben Carter was guiding him. The boy said he remembered Newton taking him and his daddy hunting. Newton asked about his daddy, and Richardson said he passed away a few years ago and that he inherited his membership in the club. They sat there and talked about old times a few minutes. Newton said he didn't remember how many times he had carried them.

Mrs. Chappell and Miss Sudie Jones did the cooking. He said they really fed them good. Newton said the first year he and Nicholas had a room over the kitchen. When it was time for them to get up, Miss Sudie would bang on the ceiling with a broomstick and holler up there, "Boys it's time to get up!"

After the first year, Mr. Chappell fixed up the guides' quarters, and they stayed there. It had a big room downstairs and two or three rooms upstairs. Cecil Brickhouse had a room in a building on the north side of the kitchen, and he said Mr. and Mrs. Chappell may have stayed there, too.

In 1960, he said there were seldom more than four members and/or guests there at a time. The members who stayed there were all northerners. The Chathams and Haneses were members then, but they and their guests stayed and ate at Dew's Island. There were only about ten members of the club then.

Newton said the Chathams and Haneses didn't hunt Currituck Club if the northern members were there. If there were no northern members there, John Wright Jr. (superintendent of Dew's Island Club) would bring Hugh and Dick Chatham and Gordon and Phillip Hanes—or a combination of them if they had guests—over to Currituck Club in the gas boat *Mildew*. There he would pick up Newton and Nicholas with two skiffs and decoys and tow them to the ponds. Then John Jr. would come back at lunchtime and pick them up.

Newton said the *Mildew* had to be the best gas boat Mr. Pat O'Neal ever built, because if John Jr. started hitting a shoal, he would just push the throttle wide open and grind it on across it.

Newton said that when he went there Mr. Cornelius Mitchell was the oldest member of the club. His address in 1939 (which I got from my Daddy's files) was 350 Madison Avenue, New York City. He said Mr. Mitchell bought a Dodge power wagon and sent it down to Currituck Club. They could use it to haul gas in drums from the mainland or wood or whatever they needed to haul. When Mr. Mitchell came down, it was parked at the end of the building, and nobody touched it because it was for his exclusive use. It was his.

There were also a couple of old Jeep station wagons over there, too. They had a wood saw down there under one of those sheds. It had a big saw blade that was turned with a Model A Ford motor with a wide belt. Mr. Chappell had somebody on the mainland cut the wood into fireplace lengths. They had to cut that up in little pieces and split it up to go in the little stoves in the bedrooms.

Newton said the second year he was there, 1961, the houseman or janitor, Wayne Jones, quit, and Newton got Graham Keaton the job. They were now staying in the guides' quarters. Up until this point, they didn't have anything to do nights except play set back. Cecil Brickhouse taught them how to do that, and he said they had some hot games. When Graham came, he brought a television.

Newton said the members would come down to the guides' quarters on evenings and associate with them just long enough to see what the weather was going to be the next day.

The guides always ate in the kitchen, and they fed them first. The northerners ate their ducks rare, and there was some kind of sauce they wanted put over them that was made out of black pea soup.

Mrs. Chappell got most of her groceries from Mr. Jerry Bunch's store at Poplar Branch Landing. When she got her groceries that day, either Mr. Jerry forgot to put the black pea soup in the bag or Mrs. Chappell forgot to get it. Either way, she didn't have it, so there was nothing to do but for Newton and Nicholas to go across the sound to Mr. Jerry's store and get the soup.

Newton had a little boat that Oscar Wilson Roberts helped him build with a seventy-five-horsepower Johnson outboard motor on it. They took that and were at Poplar Branch Landing at Mr. Jerry's store in ten minutes.

Poplar Branch Landing. *Courtesy Levie Bunch Jr.*

There was a big gas sign down there by the fish houses at Poplar Branch Landing that they kept lit, so they had no problem finding the landing going over. When they got ready to go back, it was a different story. It was pitch-dark, and the only thing they could see was Bear Head Beacon, which was right straight out from Poplar Branch Landing. When you get to Bear Head, you have to bear off to the right, then go down a ways and then bear left to get lined up with the dock at Currituck Club. After they passed Bear Head, they kept running until they could see the outline of the marsh. Soon they were back to Bear Head Beacon. Well, they must have missed their turn and just made a circle, so they went through the process again. Same thing: right back to Bear Head Beacon. There was another problem now. They had turned off the sign light at Poplar Branch Landing. Newton said, "Nicholas, we got to do sumpon different. We got to do some better lining up. There's the lighthouse." Nicholas asked, "What lighthouse?" Newton said, "How many lighthouses do you think you can see from here, Nicholas? Currituck Beach Lighthouse."

Nicholas was about to get worried. He said, "You know you get that feeling when you don't know where you're at?...When we leave Bear Head this time

Poplar Branch Landing, showing the barge that Norman Gregory used to haul coal in bags, firewood and corn to Monkey Island, Whalehead, Currituck and Pine Island Clubs. *Courtesy Carl Ross.*

Mr. Jerry Bunch's store at Poplar Branch Landing. *Courtesy Olive Bunch Butt.*

we ain't turning no more 'til we hit the marsh at Fosters up there." They ran until they almost ran aground, and they could see the marsh. They followed the marsh around until they could see the light on the end of Currituck Club dock. Newton said the light on the end of that dock looked some kinda' good that night. He said they didn't pull that trick anymore.

Another one of the members of Currituck Club—Mr. Barbour, also from New York City—would come first to Barbour's Hill Club, which was up in the False Cape area on the beach in Virginia and belonged to the Barbour family. He would stay there about two weeks, and then they would have to go up there in the power wagon and get him and bring him to Currituck Club. He lost everything he had in the stock market crash in 1929, but he made it back after things got better.

One time, Newton had a man named Webb and a friend of his out there hunting. Webb was a younger man and was telling his friend that if he could just find something to hunt one month out of the year—and Newton couldn't remember what month that was—he could hunt every month of the year. He was telling his friend about hunting all over the world.

Newton said that Canvasback and Old House were the two major ponds they hunted. When you are going up Sanders Creek, Old House is the first pond you come to on your left, right in front of the guardhouse. Canvasback was the biggest pond. It was around by Fosters Lead. Then there were some smaller ponds. Two of them were Jones pond and Mid Mossy, and then around on the outside you went across Wills Bay and came to Wills Island, and there was also a Large Wills Island pond and a Little Wills Island pond.

They killed mostly mallard, widgeon, gadwell, black ducks and blackheads. The blackheads would come late in the afternoon from Dew's Island. You could hear them coming before you could see them. They'd come in there so fast they couldn't stop; they'd swoop up over the blind, swing around and then come back in and put her down. To kill pintail, they had to go up on the beach south of the clubhouse at Cow Island Point. They traded down that shore. He didn't know, but they may have been coming up from Pine Island.

Newton said at the end of the season, when nobody else was coming, Mr. Chappell would let him and Nicholas go in Old House pond one evening late. They knew the game wardens would be watching them, being the last of the season. He said there was a back way out of Old House pond around by Fosters, so early in the day they took his boat around there and left it. When they left from the clubhouse that afternoon, they went up Sanders Creek just like normal. They saw the game wardens watching them.

As soon as they got in the blind, Nicholas started breaking down the rushes in front of the blind. Newton said, "Nicholas, what are you doing? They'll see us." Nicholas said, "They ain't going to see us; they'll be coming in so fast it ain't going to make no difference." Nicholas knew how low and fast the ducks would come from working at Dew's Island. Nicholas said, "You need to stand up and lay your gun across the top of the blind because you ain't going to have time to stand up and put it to your shoulder. When they come, they're going to be here." All of a sudden, Newton said, "What's that?" Nicholas said, "Get ready." About that time, they said *swish* and they were gone. They were going so fast you couldn't have shot them if you wanted to. They circled around and came back and put her down. They kept doing that until the dead ducks were drifting out of the decoys, and the blackheads were stooling to them until they drifted so far out of range they had to quit shooting. He said he didn't know how many they killed, but they got out of there. He said they never did tell Mr. Chappell how many they killed.

Graham Keaton

Currituck Club from 1961 to 1965

In 1961, a vacancy became available at Currituck Club for a janitor or houseman. Newton Hampton got Graham Keaton the job.

He had to get up and start building the fires in each of the members' rooms by 5:00 a.m. so it would be warm when the man got up. Then he built the fire in the fireplace in the clubroom. He kept that going all day and until they went to bed at night.

After the men got out of the house to go hunting, he would fill up all the wood boxes in the rooms. About 4:30 p.m., he'd go back upstairs and build the fires in the rooms again. He'd keep them going until the men went to bed; they'd cut the draft off and it would smolder until about one or two o'clock in the morning.

At supper time, he had to open half a dozen oysters for each member as an appetizer. If they were going to take any ducks home with them, he had to "draw" them, as they called it, which was just pulling the guts out of them. He said they didn't even want the blood washed out—just leave them like that.

If they wanted ducks served at the club, of course, he had to pick them.

After the first year, a guide's position became available, and he got that and guided the next two years. He said there was a Mr. Baker who came who had a wooden leg. He didn't seem to like Graham and Newton too much. He told Mr. Chappell he wanted Cecil Brickhouse for his exclusive guide.

Bedroom at Currituck Club.
Courtesy Fred Dunstan.

Baker was the one who said all he wanted to shoot was what he called "quality ducks," and what he considered quality ducks were greenhead mallards and black ducks. He was in the advertising business. When electric razors came out, he was the one who came up with the ad that said it would shave the fuzz off a peach. Graham couldn't remember if it was Remington or Schick.

He said when they killed their limit, that was it. They were ready to come in. Sometimes they'd go up on the beach late in the afternoon and shoot geese.

Graham said Mr. Baker always wanted to go up to Ware Creek, because that's where he said the quality ducks were.

Graham said one day that the sound was froze up, and there was a bunch of geese on the ice right down there by the dock. Mr. Chappell had gone down to Pine Island. Graham, Newton and Cecil decided to sneak down there and shoot them geese. Somebody had to go get them. Graham was

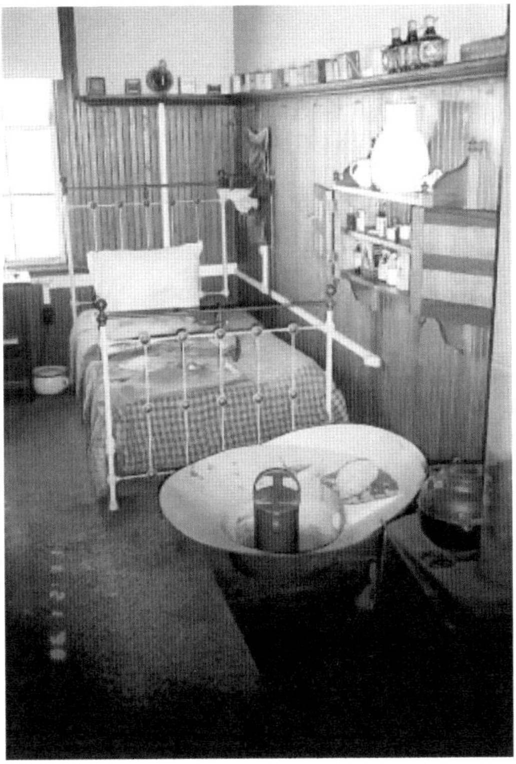

Bedroom at Currituck Club. Note the chamber pot. *Courtesy Fred Dunstan.*

elected. About the time he got to them the ice broke, and he fell in to his waist and the water was ice-cold. He got the geese and brought them back. They didn't want Mr. Chappell to know about it, so they ran on up to the house and warmed up. Graham said he didn't change his clothes. He said they had a chance to go to the ponds up on the beach, and he stayed up there and dried out. He said it was cold but he made it.

Graham said Mr. Cornelius Mitchell was a nice old man. He told Graham that his family owned twenty-seven acres in New York City. Even divided up among heirs, there was a lot of rent income there. One evening, Graham went up to Mr. Mitchell's room about 4:30 p.m. to build a fire in his stove. He didn't know the old man was in the bed. Graham said it woke him up, and he hollered like he'd been shot it startled him so bad.

Carl Ross

Sixth Superintendent of Currituck Shooting Club

The following are the recollections Carl Ross had of Currituck Shooting Club while he was superintendent.

He said Ralph Hanes, owner of Hanes Dye and Finishing Company, bought four memberships in the late '50s or early '60s. He gave memberships to his two sons-in-law, Caulder Wombel and Tommy Chatham, and one to his son, Phillip Hanes.

The club members didn't really put a value on the land until 1968 or '69, when Carl White convinced the members to sell their oceanfront property. He told them they could invest the money from the sale of the property and never have to pay any more dues.

They gave Mr. Carl an option on the property, and he sold it to Walter Davis for $1.3 million. Walter Davis was originally from Elizabeth City, North Carolina, but at this time lived in Midland, Texas. He was vice-president of Occidental Petroleum. He later sold the property to James Johnson, and Johnson developed it into what you know today as Ocean Sands.

When you divide $1.3 million by twelve members, that's right much money. At that time, many of the northerners said they'd take their money and get out. There was one southerner who got out, too: Frank Wellingham, a friend of the Haneses. He had a textile mill in Winston-Salem. By now, they had established a price of $75,000 for a membership. They sold Wellingham's interest to Jack Camp.

By the time Carl Ross got there in 1977, the Chathams and Haneses pretty well controlled the club. Hugh Chatham was president at the time, and he is the one who hired Carl Ross.

Hugh Chatham told Carl that the first time he went to Currituck Club, which was in the early 1960s, his wife Mary was with him, and she had to wait outside on the porch. He said Mr. Barbara and some of the older members were there, and it was a club rule that no women were to come in the club.

I was telling Carl that John Wright Jr. told me that they banned women in the early days, and after the Chathams and Haneses got in, they banned kids. Carl asked if I knew why they banned kids, but I didn't. He said Ralph Wombel, who is Caulder Wombel's son, was over there with his daddy.

Mr. Richardson, from Staten Island, New York, was there. He was head of St. Paul Fire and Marine Insurance Company. He rubbed the top of Ralph Wombel's head and said, "Son where did you get all that red hair?" He said, "Same place you got that bald head you son of a bitch." That was it; nobody under eighteen was allowed after that. Carl said it stayed that way up until the last few years he was there. Then people wanted to bring their families, and the club needed the per diem.

It changed from the northerners to the North Carolinians before Mr. Chappell died in 1977. Carl said that after the northerners got out, Mr. Chappell quit three times, and they hired him back each time.

When Mr. Chappell went there in 1960, the place was really in bad shape. Mr. Chappell himself would dig under the house to replace termite-eaten sills or whatever needed doing. Mr. Carl White told him the club didn't hire him to do the work himself; they hired him to see that it was done. Mr. Chappell said, "Well, the club doesn't have the money."

When Carl Ross got there, they didn't do anything for about three years, and then Gordon Hanes took over as president. Carl said the cedar shakes on the outside of the building were so thin you could almost stick your finger through them. Gordon Hanes personally provided the money to have the cedar shakes replaced. They also replaced the cedar shingle roof. Carl said he took the shingles off the roof, and on the back of them was stamped "South Mills Shingle Company." He said they had been there since 1879.

Carl said he thought the problem Mr. Chappell was having was when the southerners were taking over and wanted change and there were still some northerners who didn't want change.

When Mr. Chappell went there in 1960, there were no bathrooms. They took a bedroom upstairs, and he made a bathroom out of it. Mr. Chatham paid for it, and they called it "Chatham Hall." In 1967, they took another room downstairs under Chatham Hall and made another bathroom. They had to have a New York meeting to do that.

The superintendent of a membership club has a struggle, because the members generally own their own businesses or they are captains of industry and are all used to calling the shots. Mr. Carl White never had to deal with that at Pine Island or Narrows Island. The only two people he ever had to deal with were Mr. Barney and Mr. Slick. Mr. Carl's daddy, John T. White, had members to deal with when he was superintendent of Narrows Island Club.

When Carl was there, it was the first year after Mr. Chappell died, and Mrs. Chappell went back there as cook. She had Mary Margaret Scarborough and Dorothy Midgett Tredwell helping her. Dorothy's husband, Al Tredwell, was a guide. Other guides were Elmer Merrell, Nob Bunch, Garland Evans, Joe Scarborough and Forest Walker, who had just retired as a federal marshal and wanted a job around the water.

I can't begin to name all the people who have worked at Currituck Club. In addition to the ones I've already named, I know that Tilman Merrell was a marsh guard and guide there. Booty Spruill worked there. Levie Bunch Jr. worked there. In later years, Walton Carter guided there, as did his sons, Ben and Clay. Mike Sawyer guided there some. My grandson, Chandler Sawyer, guided there a few days, as did so many more I don't know.

I need to stop here and tell the story that Janet Rose Ferrell Ross told me about how she and Carl Ross got married. Janet was married to Richie Ferrell. They had two children, Chad and Allison. Richie died from cancer when he was forty-three years old. Janet was teaching school at the time. Carl Ross was separated from his wife, Debbie Jones Ross. They had two daughters, Pam and Andrea, who were with their mother. Long story short, Carl started seeing Janet, and soon Janet quit teaching school, went to work cooking at Currituck Club and took her kids with her. Chad was thirteen and Allison was eight.

On December 15, 1999, Janet got up as usual, cooked breakfast for the men and got them ready to go hunting. She put the kids on the boat to go to school. Then she cleaned up, started lunch and got it where she could leave it.

She and Carl got in the car and drove around to Currituck Courthouse, and Carl got his divorce; then they walked into the Register of Deeds Office and got their marriage license. They met Mr. Charles Wellons at Coinjock Baptist Church (he was pastor there). Bobby and Dot Henley and Walton Carter were there as witnesses. Carter had his hip boots on. They went back to Currituck Club, and she fixed lunch for the men. Everything went on as usual, and nobody knew what had taken place!

Now back to the story. Carl said that Gordon Hanes came down there one day and said, "We're going to clean this place up." Carl said, "Yes sir, what do you want done?" He said to get rid of the smokehouse and two or three other little buildings that were there. "Get rid of the cistern; we don't need that. Get rid of the guides' quarters." Carl said, "I just put a brand-new shower in it." Hanes said, "I don't care; get rid of it. I want to put a new clay road in here so I don't get stuck." Carl got Eddie Younts to clean the road up and put the clay in there.

Carl asked Eddie if he would help him tear those buildings down so he could burn them up. Eddie said, "You let me handle that." He sold the guides' quarters to Hiriam Mayo, a lawyer in Washington, North Carolina. I sold Hiriam a lot on Persimmon Street in Corolla Village for $50,000. I didn't own the lot; I was the broker. They got Julian Bray to move the guides' quarters from Currituck Club to Corolla Village. Hiriam has since

Carl and Janet Ross in duck blind. *Courtesy Carl Ross.*

James Guard and Alex Ross at Burris's guard camp. *Courtesy Carl Ross.*

sold it, but it's still there. The present owner is Ann Snyder; we call her "Ann the Artist."

When Carl got to Currituck Club, he saw that Mr. Chappell had gotten little aluminum boats with six-horsepower motors. They were lighter to pull over the dyking to the ponds than the old juniper skiffs. You still had to pull them to the ponds with a gas boat.

The gas boats they had were two flat-bottom boats with box tunnels and six-cylinder Chevrolet motors hooked up straight (no transmission). They had cabins. Mr. Johnnie Guard built them. They had another wide flat-bottom boat with a tunnel and a cabin they called the *Broad Bill*. It had a V8 Ford motor in it. Then they had the *Miss Dare*, which was a former game warden boat. Mr. Pat O'Neal had built that with a concave tunnel in it for the North Carolina Wildlife Resources Commission.

When Carl Ross left Currituck Club in 2001, his brother, Alex Ross, took over as superintendent and still has that job as of this writing.

After the club burned down in 2003, they elected not to rebuild on the beach. They developed the land where the club had been located. Until 2008, they rented a cottage on the beach during the hunting season. In 2009, they worked a deal with Carl Ross to use a house on the mainland near his landing.

The 1971-1972 Hunting Season at Currituck Club

As Told by Levie Bunch Jr.

When Levie Bunch was a young boy—in fact so young his daddy wouldn't let him have a gun—and he only had a row skiff, Mr. Chappell gave him a dozen cork decoys. Levie said he and Otis Parker went out back of his grandaddy's (Jerry Bunch's) store and took a blowtorch and blackened them. Otis told him that was the way they did it years ago. After he had blackened them, he sat them out in the yard a few days. They were factory cork decoys. Some were canvasback, redheads or other species, but they made black ducks out of all of them.

His granddaddy had a blind close to shore at Poplar Branch Landing. Levie and his cousin, Butch Caroon, would take his rowboat, those decoys and a few geese and tie out in that blind. Playing duck hunting. I can understand that, because when I was a kid, I made me a boat out of a dry goods box, put it in a big ditch in the pasture and stuck some pine bushes around it for a blind. I had three or four decoys that my granddaddy had, and I would play duck hunting.

When Levie got a little older, he asked Mr. Chappell if he'd sell him a bag or two of decoys. Mr. Chappell told him he couldn't sell him any because they belonged to the club but that he could give him some for the wheels, shafts and rudders he had given the club and wouldn't take any pay for.

Mr. Chappell told him to come on and they'd take the *Dare*, go over to the club and see what they could find. In the bunch Mr. Chappell gave him were three Ned Burgess widgeon. After Mr. Chappell died, Levie gave Mrs. Chappell one of those widgeon. He still has the other two as of this writing.

Levie worked for Mr. Chappell at Currituck Club in the 1971–72 hunting season, and then he went into the Coast Guard.

He said one day that Mr. Chappell and several of the guides were sitting around the dinner table eating, and Mr. Chappell said, "Levie, how would you like to run the *Dare*?" (This was the nice gas boat that Mr. Pat O'Neal had built for the North Carolina Wildlife Resources Commission for a game warden boat. When they went to fiberglass boats, Mr. Chappell bought the *Dare* for Currituck Club.)

Levie said, "You're just messing with me. You ain't gonna let me use the *Dare*."

"Have I ever told you I was gonna do something I didn't do?"

"No sir you haven't."

"Well what am I gonna start doing it now for? You're gonna have to take Mr. Payne and Mr. Richardson."

When he said that, Joe Scarborough was sitting at the other end of the table and started snickering. Levie looked up at him and said, "Something's up here." Mr. Chappell said, "You know Mr. Richardson. He calls you dock master at Poplar Branch Landing. He liked you and you liked him. Mr. Payne is just as nice a man as Mr. Richardson. You can use the *Dare* for a week, and you are gonna take them hunting for a week."

Levie said he got in early from hunting one day, and he looked down the dock; Mr. Chappell had come in from Poplar Branch with these two men (Payne and Richardson). The first one was Mr. Richardson, and behind him was this great big man. Levie said he weighed over five hundred pounds. Levie said to himself, "Oh my God." He said he knew his eyes were big as hen eggs. Mr. Chappell was about twenty feet behind them down the dock, and when he saw Levie's expression, he started doing a little dance, and of course the men couldn't see him. Levie said he was about to die. How in the world was he going to get that big man in one of those little aluminum boats?

The next day, when they got ready to go hunting, Levie got him in the *Dare* all right because it had steps to get down in the boat. The procedure was to take the gas boats and tow the skiffs to the ponds.

When they got to the pond and got ready to get Mr. Payne in the aluminum boat, that was a different story. He said he and Mr. Richardson got on the opposite side and tried to balance it up. He said they made it but that the boat only had about three and a half inches of freeboard. They were at

Mid Mossy pond. He had a ring of keys, and not one would fit the gate. Mr. Richardson told him to leave them there and for him to take the *Dare* to get the marsh guard to open the gate. Levie told him he hated to leave them there, but Mr. Richardson told him to go on and that they would be all right.

Levie went and got Elmer Merrell, the marsh guard, and he came and unlocked the gate and they went in. He said they hunted the whole week, and they didn't have any more incidents.

Some of the people who worked at Currituck Club when Levie was there included Linwood Tillet, Ronnie Midgett, Randy Barnard and Joe Scarborough. The marsh guards were Elmer Merrell, Ed Cartwright and George Smith. Smith lived in the guard camp and just went home to Kitty Hawk on Saturday afternoons and came back on Sunday afternoons. The marsh guards did all the feeding.

Levie Jr. had the foresight from an early age to see the historical value of the nautical things that people were throwing away, and he collected them,

Levie Bunch Jr. at the end of Penn's Wharf in Waterlily. This is where I and many other people who belonged to Coinjock Baptist Church were baptized in the 1940s. My grandmother, Carrie Boswood, thought it was all right for me to join Pilmoor Memorial Methodist Church at Currituck, where my wife Frances belonged, since I'd been baptized in Currituck Sound. *Courtesy Levie Bunch Jr.*

including old boats. He has the finest private collection of old boats that I know of. He has been very generous in donating things to the Whalehead Preservation Trust, including two shad boats built in the early 1900s by Otis Doe in Wanchese.

I left Monkey Island in January 1979 at the end of the hunting season. The Nature Conservancy had purchased the property but no personal property. Mr. Frank Penn told me to back my barge up there and take anything I wanted. I did take most of the furniture but felt like I should leave one room original. I left the dining room. Had I known it was going to be taken over by the birds, I would have taken everything. When I left, Levie Bunch Jr. came to Monkey Island to look after it for the Nature Conservancy until it gave it to the U.S. Fish and Wildlife Service. When he left, he was smart enough to clean out what I didn't take.

Narrows Island Club

I wrote the history of Narrows Island Club for the Currituck County Historical Society in 1976. I think for me to repeat that history is the best way for me to start with Narrows Island.

The idea of Narrows Island Club was first conceived by a man named E.E. Pray. He came to New York in the summer of 1881. He had bought land and had options to purchase lands in Currituck and Dare Counties in North Carolina and wanted to organize a group of duck hunters to take over these holdings from him.

The club was organized with twenty-four charter members. At a meeting held on July 22, 1881, G.G. Manger was elected president. Mr. Pray had already employed Major E.H. Bailey of North Carolina to represent himself and the club on the grounds. That fall, a number of the members visited a settlement on Currituck Sound then known as Van Slyke's Landing and for that season occupied a house belonging to H.H. Halstead. Van Slyke's Landing was reached in a number of ways by the members. One came by tugboat to Coinjock and then by cart to Van Slyke's Landing.

The following year, they made arrangements to occupy Van Slyke's house near the landing, and they used this until 1884. At that time, the clubhouse was completed and occupied on Narrows Island. In 1884, the club purchased the Walker marshes and Brant Island.

Original Narrows Island Clubhouse from the back side. The little boy is Carl White; his sister, Pearl, is standing behind him. His mother is on his right. *Courtesy Carl Ross.*

Captain E.H. Ryder of Long Island was employed as superintendent of the club in 1883. In the summer of 1891, Captain Ryder was killed by lightning while riding in a boat in the Little Narrows. Ashley Corbell was appointed to fill his place.

In 1894, some of the residents of Powells Point asked permission to cut a canal through the Devil's Elbow in the Little Narrows, but the request was denied.

The club had a lot of trouble with the natives poaching and threatening the marsh guards. In January 1895, Apollos Owens, a marsh guard at Burroughs, came to the Narrows Island Club House about nine o'clock at night in a high state of alarm. After that, they put two guards at Burroughs.

In September 1895, they decided to purchase corn for baiting, and this apparently was the first time baiting was practiced.

In 1897, Currituck Club and Narrows Island Club had a dispute over some property. An agreement was reached whereby Thoroughfare Island belonging to Currituck Club was exchanged for the Dowdy's pond tract.

At the annual meeting in 1903, Mr. Trotter reported what had been done in the way of purchasing maps to be presented to the high school at Poplar Branch.

In past years, many members had regretted the lack of education among the population of Poplar Branch, and some of them had made efforts to induce their boatmen to learn to read and write, but there were practically no schools in the communities on the mainland. Two or three years before 1903, Mr. Trotter had taken up this matter with S.M. Beasley and Colonel Woodhouse, and P.Y. Poyner had kept the thing going and laid the foundation for the good school now in operation in Poplar Branch. Following Trotter, W.H. Weelock took up the work with interest and for years carried it forward with great success.

Above: The old Narrows Island Clubhouse from the front. Note observation tower on the top of the house so they could look out over the marsh. This clubhouse was located in the Little Narrows. When Mr. Slick bought the Narrows Island property he built the house that is there now on this same spot. *Courtesy Archie Johnson and Bud Coppedge.*

Right: Original Narrows Island boat dock. Rudie White, Mr. Carl White's wife, in door. In the skiff are Laura White and Carl and Rudie White's daughters Catherine and Audrey White. *Courtesy Carl Ross.*

Carl White in house pond at Narrows Island Club. *Courtesy Carl Ross.*

About this time, the members were coming to Snowden Station by train and then by cart to Van Slyke's Landing (now known as Poplar Branch). In 1909, the club bought a motorboat so the members could be picked up at Munden's Point and carried to the club. They came this way for several years.

About 1910, Ashley Corbell died, and John T. White was appointed superintendent. Mr. White was the father of Carl P. White, who was later superintendent of Pine Island Club for thirty-eight years and superintendent of Narrows Island Club from 1968 until he died in 1975.

In 1923, Mr. John T. White resigned as superintendent, and Mr. Cleveland Aydlett was appointed in his place.

The logbook indicates they had both good and bad years hunting back in those days, just as we have now. In 1907–8, they killed 1,475 birds, and in 1909–10, they had a total of 3,210.

The members are too numerous to mention here but included Ashbel H. Barney, Charles T. Barney, George F. Dominick, David Dows Jr., Samuel W. Fairchild, Frederick C. Havemeyer and William Rockfellow. The last members were Lucius H. Beers, Charles A. Cass, William T. Brown, John R. Montgomery, W.T. Sampson Smith, James M. Symington and George DeForest Loard. All of these men were from New York, with the exception of Symington, who was from Newark, New Jersey.

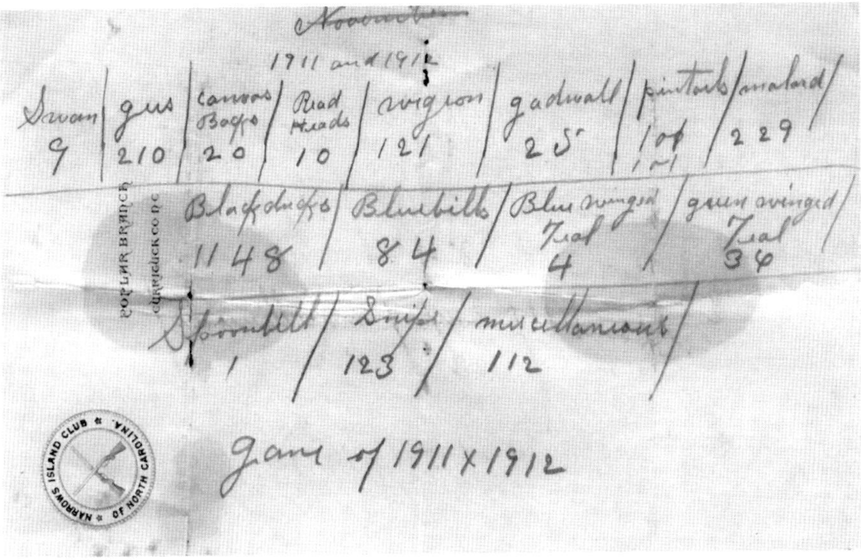

Record of game killed at Narrows Island Club in the 1911–12 season. *Courtesy Carl Ross.*

On March 9, 1940, a meeting of the members of Narrows Island Club was held at Currituck Courthouse, in the office of the organization's attorney, Chester Morris. At this meeting, the Executive Committee approved the transfer and conveyance of all real property in Currituck County, North Carolina, to the Currituck Shooting Club. The agreement between the two clubs provided that the present members of the Narrows Island Club could reserve from the assets any or all of the books, prints, pictures and household furniture. The balance of the personal property was to go to Currituck Club.

In looking over the old club rules, I found a couple of interesting points. One, no employee was allowed to hunt on the property, and secondly, no pump or automatic gun was allowed.

In 1945, Currituck Shooting Club leased the property known as the Narrows Island Club property to O.L. Woodhouse of Grandy, North Carolina. This lease included Brant Island, Grandy's Island and Narrows Island home marshes.

In 1950, Currituck Shooting Club sold all the Narrows Island Club property with the exception of Brant Island and Burris's to Mr. Burch, who employed Richmond Outlaw as caretaker. Mr. Burch kept the property five or six years and then sold it to P.K. Gravley of Rocky Mount, North Carolina, who was a top executive of China American Tobacco Company.

Tram road at Narrows Island Club used to take supplies from the dock to the clubhouse. Lydia, Audrey and John T. White. *Courtesy Carl Ross.*

After Mr. Gravley's death, Carl White and O.L. Woodhouse leased the marsh in 1967 and employed Melvin Dowdy as caretaker. Mr. White and Mr. Woodhouse then negotiated the sale for the property between the Gravley heirs and Earl Slick of Winston-Salem, North Carolina, who still owns the property as of this writing. Mr. Carl had the connection with Mr. Slick because he had hunted at Pine Island, and Mr. Woodhouse had the connection with the Gravley heirs.

I could not write this history of Narrows Island without telling of it as I know it today. I can remember going through the Little Narrows and seeing the old club dock just a mass of weathered piles, the old rail tracks that carried supplies and baggage from the dock to the club just lying hidden in tall grass in abandonment. Today, it is a great pleasure to ride through these same waters and see the lodge Mr. Earl Slick has built. It is a modest house compared to many of the old clubhouses, but the bulkheads, dock and lawn are kept in immaculate condition.

There is a pond just to the south of the house where you can see ducks flying in and out most anytime you pass. They raise more ducks at Narrows Island than they kill. I remember one time seeing a wild goose eat grass out of the hands of the caretaker, Leslie Jones.

Old Narrows Island Boathouse. *Courtesy Carl Ross.*

Gloria Dowdy has cooked for the Slick family for over thirty years. *Author's collection.*

Narrows Island Clubhouse as it is today. *Courtesy Carl Ross.*

Narrows Island Club boathouse as it is today. *Courtesy Carl Ross.*

My impression of Mr. Slick, who owns Narrows Island and Pine Island, is that he is a man like many before him—someone who came to Currituck and fell in love with what he found here. He wants to protect the natural resources he found and leave them a little better than he found them.

I received the information for the history of Narrows Island from the following sources: a book of the bylaws that contained the names of the members and the history up to 1923; the records of the late Chester Morris, who was their attorney at one time; talking to Mr. Orville Woodhouse and Caleb Poyner (Richmond Outlaw's stepson); and from personal experience.

Earl F. Slick

Earl Slick was a man like J.P. Knapp and many other wealthy men who came to Currituck for the ducks and liked what they found. They wanted to help preserve what they had found for generations to come. Not only did they help preserve the duck habitat, but they also helped with the schools, library and many other things. So much has been written about Mr. Knapp that I won't get into that.

Mr. Slick was also a large benefactor to the Whalehead Preservation Trust, and the Slick Foundation still helps the trust. He contributed to many other things locally, in both Currituck and Dare Counties, but he always remained in the background. He didn't want publicity for what he did. He gave the Audubon Society five miles of the sound side of the Pine Island Property beach and the marsh, as well as some oceanfront and Pine Island Clubhouse. They took control of it on January 1, 2010.

To tell you a little about the man who most people only knew as Earl Slick I will quote from his obituary:

> *He was born in Clarion, Pennsylvania, the son of Tom Baker Slick and Bernice Frates Urschel, and grew up in Oklahoma City, Oklahoma. During World War II, he served as a pilot in the U.S. Army Corps. Following the war, he founded Slick Airways, the first nationwide air freight business. He*

Earl F. Slick. *Courtesy Phyllis S. Cowell.*

and his brother also pursued their father's groundbreaking business in oil exploration and discovery.

Mr. Slick and his wife, Jane, moved to Winston-Salem in 1952 from San Antonio, Texas. Whenever asked about his profession, he would jokingly reply "dog trainer"; however, he did enjoy a varied business career including investments in broadcasting, aircraft operations, hospitality, ranching and real estate. He served as a member of the Winston-Salem Planning Board and on the boards of a number of local charitable organizations including Old Salem, Summit School, and North Carolina Baptist Hospital. Together with his brother and sister, he was also very active in support of the Southwest Foundation for Biomedical Research in San Antonio, Texas. He, with his family, endowed the Slick Foundation as a surviving legacy of his philanthropy.

He enjoyed reading, travel, tennis, outdoor activities, good food and, of course, his dogs. His loyal friend, Buddy, will miss him.

He had a great love for the outdoors. He enjoyed riding horses, fishing and hunting, particularly the elusive quail in Georgia and fast-flying ducks on North Carolina's Outer Banks. It was his love which inspired his support for conservation efforts.

Carl White first introduced me to Mr. Slick in 1973 or '74. In 1974, I represented the Monkey Island Investment Company—which comprised

Earl Slick, Winston-Salem, North Carolina; Joe and Rex Frates, Tulsa, Oklahoma; and Devane Clark, Dallas, Texas—in the purchase of the Monkey Island property, which consisted of the seven-acre Monkey Island, with clubhouse, and three miles of Currituck Beach from sound to ocean.

I opened Monkey Island Club as a joint venture with the Monkey Island Investment Company—the first time it had ever been open to the public since it was started in 1876.

After a year, the Monkey Island Investment Company wanted out of the deal. I was told that the Frateses were the second-largest holders of office space in the country at the time, and office space was going begging. Mr. Penn gave them 150 acres from sound to ocean for the money they had paid down on the property. I understand Mr. Slick took his partners out of the deal.

I ran Monkey Island Club for three more years as a joint venture with Frank Penn in the process of selling it again.

One day, I was riding Mr. Slick and the Frateses up the beach in my old jeep. This was before anything was built on the beach. You could look as far as you could see and just see white sand, gold sea oats and blue ocean and sky. Rex Frates wanted to stop and pick up a conch shell. There were a lot of them washed up on the beach. Mr. Slick said, "If you want to pick up conch shells, I own sixty miles of them in Australia. You can pick up all you want there."

Before Mr. Slick decided to develop the Pine Island property, he was going to sell what we call the south mile, which was in Dare County. It's what you know today as the development of Sanderling.

I put Mr. Slick in touch with a man in New York City named George Horn. Mr. Slick went to New York and met him in the Blue Room of the St. Regis Hotel. They didn't make a deal, but when Mr. Slick got home he called me and said he was impressed with Mr. Horn.

Mr. Slick knew that I had successfully developed Corolla Village for Carl White, Kenyon Wilson and Stewart Hume. He stopped by my office on occasion to talk about the best way to develop the south mile, but most of the time if he wanted to talk to me he would tell me to come to Pine Island or Narrows Island. He gave me his home telephone number and told me to call him anytime I had anything to talk about. I never did call him at home, though.

When Mr. Slick decided to develop the south mile, Carl White owned the old Caffey's Inlet Coast Guard Station along with eight hundred feet from sound to ocean.

Carl White died, and Mr. Slick and Miss Rudie, Carl's wife, both had enough faith in my judgment that they agreed they would abide by what I said was a fair trade of land on the south of the White property for the eight hundred feet with the old Coast Guard station.

Mr. Slick wanted to restore the station into what is now the Sanderling Inn Restaurant. He spent a lot of money restoring it, and it was not a paying thing at first, but as Bill Hollan told me, the numbers didn't have to work if Mr. Slick wanted to do it.

I didn't have the close relationship with Mr. Slick that the local people who worked for him did, but we stayed in touch over the years; in fact, he called me just a few months before he died. In this conversation, we were reminiscing, and he told me he didn't know why he couldn't see it: I could have put together twelve miles of beach, all the land from sound to ocean from Currituck Beach lighthouse to the south end of what is now Sanderling, except for the sound front of what is now the Currituck Club development, for $10 million.

I have talked to a lot of people who have worked for and cooked for the Slick family, and they all tell me how good the family has been and is to them.

William E. Hollan Jr.

I first got to know Bill Hollan about 1973. It was after Mr. Slick purchased the Pine Island property. He was in his twenties at the time and a very smart and personable young man.

He was Mr. Slick's right-hand man, so to speak, and Mr. Slick made him president of Turnpike Properties, a corporation Mr. Slick owned that owns many other companies, including the Sanderling Inn and Restaurant, the Left Bank Restaurant in Duck and the Hampton Inn at Corolla, just to name a few things. Bill was the one who looked after the development of Sanderling and Pine Island.

Bill joined Currituck Shooting Club and has been president for right many years now. After Currituck Club burned down, I wrote Bill a letter and told him I really hated to see Currituck Club die when it was the oldest duck hunting club in America in continuous operation. I told him that I knew he was the one person who could keep it together. The older members had died out, and the younger members who had inherited their fathers' shares were more interested in developing the beach.

I'm glad to say that, as of this writing, the club is still active. At first, after the fire, they rented a cottage on the beach for the hunting season, but that didn't work too well. Last year, they rented a place from Carl Ross on the mainland and went out from his landing. Time will tell what will happen.

William E. Hollan Jr. *Courtesy William E. Hollan Jr.*

Beginning of Pine Island Club, Joseph Baum's house—superintendent's house after he sold the property. *Courtesy Ernest Brickhouse.*

Superintendent's house and Pine Island Clubhouse. *Courtesy Ernest Brickhouse.*

Mr. Carl and daughter Audrey White. "Superintendent's house December 1943. Dad and I leaving had to drive around because the sound was frozen. We got stuck and had to have the Coast Guard help us. We spent the night with Granny and left the next morning." *Courtesy Carl Ross.*

Bill was president of Turnpike Properties until a few years ago, when Mr. Slick made him chairman to make room for his grandson-in-law, Allen Ives, to be president.

When I first knew Bill, he would fly down here in a little yellow Piper Cub. It didn't even have a radio. He would follow the road down here from Winston-Salem. He flew to the airstrip at Maple before it was the Currituck County Airport. There was a four-thousand-foot strip of cement the navy had there in World War II.

My Currituck Realty office is right next door to my mother's house in Coinjock. After my Daddy and grandmother died, Mama would fix dinner (lunch) and call me to come eat. Many times when she called, I really didn't have time to go up to the house and eat, but I knew she had fixed it for me

Left: Dock at Pine Island. Carl White in boat, Leslie Jones standing on dock. Audrey White fishing. *Courtesy Carl Ross.*

Below: *Left to right*: Eldridge Becham, Wiley Jones, Ernest Brickhouse, Leslie Jones, Carl White, Mr. Barney (owner of Pine Island Club). *Courtesy Ernest Brickhouse.*

Pintails on the yard at Pine Island Clubhouse. *Courtesy Laverne Brickhouse.*

Bedroom at Pine Island Club. *Courtesy Ernest Brickhouse.*

This page: Living room at Pine Island Club. *Courtesy Ernest Brickhouse.*

so I always went and took with me whoever was here in the office. Bill was with me on at least one of those occasions, and he later told me that was the first time he had ever eaten collard greens.

I have been proud to consider Bill Hollan my friend for over thirty-five years.

Clarine Doxey

Cook at Pine Island

I went to school with Clarine Doxey. I knew that she cooked at Pine Island for a long time. I called her up one day when I started writing this book and asked her if she would tell me a little of her experiences cooking at Pine Island.

Clarine said Ernest Brickhouse came to see her one day in 1985 and asked her about cooking at Pine Island. May Dunston, who had cooked there for years, was retiring, and he needed a cook. She told him she couldn't cook for those folks; she was not a gourmet cook but was just a plain country cook. Ernest said that's all they wanted. Clarine was alone. Her husband had died years earlier, and all her children were grown and gone, so she took the job.

The following is what she wrote up for me:

> *I retired from the Currituck County Sheriff's Department in 1985 and accepted a job as cook at Pine Island Hunt Club. It was a very pleasant and rewarding one. During that time I met a wide range of interesting people from all over the country during the hunting season. I was glad they liked country cooking as I was not a gourmet cook. Grilled duck breast, whole roasted ducks, collards and wild rice suited them just fine, along with cornbread and dessert. Mr. and Mrs. Slick were such nice people to work for; I could not have asked for better employers.*

Clarine Doxey, cook at Pine Island Club from 1985 until she retired in 2000. *Author's collection.*

Kitchen at Pine Island.

Dining room at Pine Island. *Courtesy Ernest Brickhouse.*

Game room at Pine Island. *Courtesy Ernest Brickhouse.*

Mr. Carl White is the one sitting back in the chair with a bald head. The others were guests. *Courtesy Ernest Brickhouse.*

The clubhouse was such a wonderful place to be a part of; it was kept in such great condition to have been built in 1913. It was admired by all those who came there to stay. Being situated away from the main road, you felt like you were in another world, away from the hustle and bustle. I still go there occasionally. I like to go at Thanksgiving and see all of the Slick family and see how the great-grandchildren have grown since the year before. I will always miss being a part of such a special place. My daughter, Patricia Leary, replaced me when I retired in 2000.

Working at Pine Island Club

As Told by Ernest Brickhouse

Mr. Carl White was superintendent when Ernest Brickhouse started working as a guide at Pine Island on November 1, 1956. It wasn't a full-time job then. When he wasn't needed at Pine Island, he worked with Ernest Lane as a finish carpenter and cabinetmaker. Charlie Dozier Sr. told me one time that Ernest Brickhouse could make a dresser drawer that would hold kerosene. That was Charlie's expression of how good of a cabinetmaker Ernest is.

When Ernest started working at Pine Island, Austin D. Barney from Hartford, Connecticut, owned the property and had owned it since 1935. They carried hunters on a commercial basis. They usually had six to eight hunters a day. The club was only open for the hunting season for about three or three and a half months per year, except for about two weeks in the summertime when Mr. and Mrs. Barney would come down. Sometimes they'd bring two guests.

Ernest's wife, Laverne, started keeping the books at Pine Island in 1956 and is still keeping them as of this writing.

Before there was a paved road, they picked up the sportsmen at Poplar Branch Landing and carried them to Pine Island by boat. There were some who wanted to drive around, and they had somebody meet them on the east side of the Sound Bridge and follow them to the club in case they got stuck. In the 1980s, after they got the road, most of the sportsmen would drive, but there were still some who preferred the boat trip.

Left to right: Ernest Brickhouse, guide; Leslie Jones, guide; Mr. Austin D. Barney, owner of Pine Island; Mr. Lefferts, guest; Mr. Garfield, guest; and Eldridge Beacham, marsh guard and guide. *Courtesy Ernest Brickhouse.*

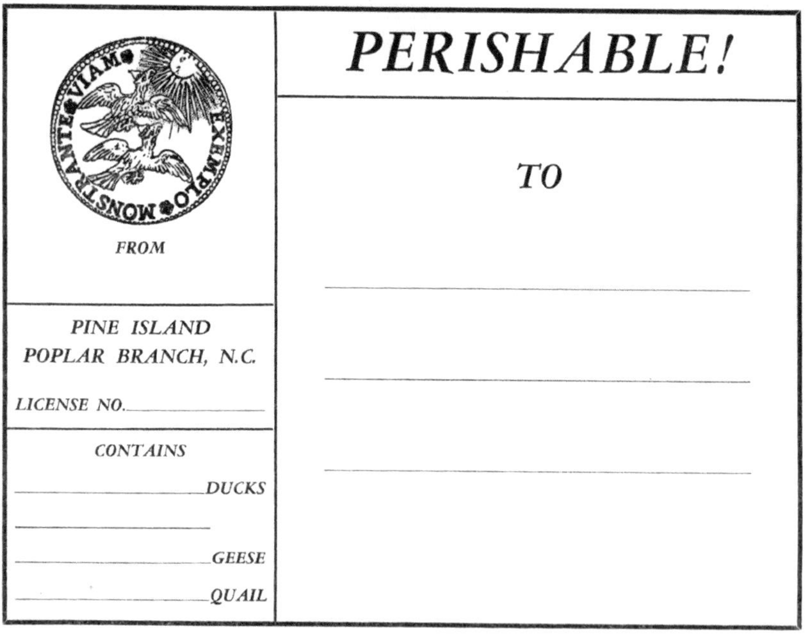

MONSTRANTE VIAM EXEMPLO

FROM

PINE ISLAND
POPLAR BRANCH, N.C.

LICENSE NO.________

CONTAINS

________ DUCKS

____

________ GEESE

________ QUAIL

PERISHABLE!

TO

____

____

____

Shipping label for game.

The superintendent's house at Pine Island Club. *Courtesy Ernest Brickhouse.*

In the kitchen of the superintendent's house. *Left to right*: Mr. Carl White, his granddaughter Phyllis Ross, Ernest Brickhouse, Miss Rudie White, Ray Wright and Carroll Merrell. *Courtesy Ernest Brickhouse.*

Drying clothes over a stove in a guide's quarters. *Left to right:* Joe Scarborough, Ernest Brickhouse and Laverne Brickhouse. *Courtesy Ernest Brickhouse.*

Back before the paved road, they had what they called the inside road. This was a sand road along the sound from Caffey's Inlet to Pine Island. Ernest said they had trouble keeping that road up because it was so much of a better road than the pole road and because a lot of folks would use that if they could get by with it; with a lot of use, it was hard to keep up.

I'll explain to you what the pole road was. The Coast Guard had a telephone line from one Coast Guard Station to the next down the beach. There were no improved roads, just tracks in the sand along by the telephone poles from Caffey's Inlet to Currituck Club. This is where we turned over to the ocean and drove the beach to Corolla or all the way up to Sandbridge, Virginia, if you wanted to go that far.

In front of Currituck Club is where the beach changed. From there south it was real pebbly, and you could get stuck easy. From there to Sandbridge, the beach was just as flat as Daytona Beach, Florida. I have a picture in my office taken in the '70s of my jeep on Daytona Beach and a picture of it on Currituck Beach, and you can't tell the difference.

Before the 1970s, there were not many people around here who had a four-wheel-drive vehicle. With a two-wheel-drive vehicle, we had to let the air in our tires down to about ten or fifteen pounds to drive the pole

The pole road. Fishermen pull a dory on a trailer to go up the beach fishing. *Courtesy Ernest Brickhouse.*

Back road along the sound side of the Pine Island property. *Courtesy Ernest Brickhouse.*

road and the beach. It was just as important to let it out of the front tires as it was the back tires. We'd do this at Caffey's Inlet. With a two-wheel-drive, you had to pick your places to stop if you wanted to get going again. To pump the tires back up, I would take a spark plug out, and I had a thing with a long hose that I could screw in there and it would pump the tires up.

Ernest said when he first went to work at Pine Island that if somebody got stuck on the beach and had to leave their car, when they came back it may not have any wheels on it—or it may not even have an engine. Nobody ever knew who stripped it. He said one got stuck behind the clubhouse one day, and the man had to leave it. When he came back to get it the next day, the wheels were gone.

The procedure for hunting at Pine Island was that you would get up and have breakfast about 7:00 a.m. and get out by 8:00 a.m.; you would be back by at least 1:00 p.m.

When Mr. Barney still owned the property, there was a Mr. Clark who came down. Ernest said he always wore a red bow tie hunting. At that time, they could go out in the marsh and get their limit of ducks in the morning and then come in, go out on the beach and shoot geese in a pond near a sand hill in the afternoon.

Wiley Jones was guiding Mr. Clark, and he said, "Well Mr. Clark, we'll go up the beach this afternoon and maybe we'll get a goose." Mr. Clark said, "Okay." They went up there and staked out some goose decoys, and they were sitting there in the blind and kept looking to the north because that's where all the geese were coming from. After a while, Wiley saw this one old goose coming, and he said, "Mr. Clark, here comes a goose, but I don't think he's coming close enough." He said, "Well, we'll just have to wait and see." The old goose was coming in a straight line; he knew where he was going. He wasn't paying a bit of attention to the decoys or their calling.

Ernest had gone up there with Wiley to help him get tied out, and they thought the goose was way out of distance to kill. Wiley said, "Mr. Clark there's no need to shoot that goose; he's way out of range." And he sort of forgot about it, and then he heard the gun go off—*bam*! He looked around, and the old goose was tumbling out. Wiley said, "Mr. Clark I can't believe that." Mr. Clark said, "Well, I kinda' thought I could kill him. I'm one of them Maryland hunters." When they got in, Wiley said, "I'm going to find out where he hit that goose." They found a number 1 buckshot right back of his head.

Boat dock at Pine Island, with a skiff-load of decoys. The skiff was built by Cleveland "Buggins" Lewark. Standing on dock is Alex Ross Sr., Mr. Carl White's son-in-law, holding his daughter, Phyllis. Note at the far end of the dock in the water is a float box used to tie in open water for redheads and canvasback. *Courtesy Carl Ross.*

Mr. Barney died sometime about 1970, and Earl Slick bought the property in 1972. He already owned Narrows Island. He bought that in 1967.

They still operated the property on a commercial basis, but they changed how they operated. They only hunted three days a week and didn't usually have over four hunters at a time. Once in a while, they would have five; then they would take a third rig. Mr. Slick had designated two-thirds of the marsh as a sanctuary or rest area in which they didn't hunt. They had an arrangement with the Currituck County Game Board that as long as they paid for the blind license they could keep the blinds but wouldn't have to hunt them, and nobody could have a blind within five hundred yards of them.

They cut down on the hunters, because after Mr. Slick set aside two-thirds of the marsh, they just didn't have the territory to hunt. They had some fields on the sound side of the beach where they planted corn and millet for the ducks and a field of sunflowers for the doves.

Above: *Left to right*: Ernest Brickhouse, Ray Wright and Judge Ward, 1994. *Courtesy Ernest Brickhouse.*

Left: Eddie Wheatley, marsh guard and guide. *Courtesy Carl Ross.*

Ernest Brickhouse in a new boat; James Lupton in an old skiff. The boat Ernest is in is a fiberglass fishing boat that Mr. Barney gave Mr. Slick when Mr. Slick bought Narrows Island. After Mr. Barney died and Mr. Slick bought Pine Island, Ernest brought the boat to Pine Island and made modifications to it; he said it made a fine icebreaker. *Courtesy Ernest Brickhouse.*

Carl White died in 1975, and Ernest Brickhouse took over as superintendent of Pine Island and Narrows Island Clubs until he retired in 1995, at which time Jeff Davenport took over as superintendent and still is as of this writing.

They kept a marsh guard camp there on Straight Creek until 1985. Ernest said when the old camp went bad he built one a little farther up the creek that was on stilts. He built it up on stilts so the guard could see all over the marsh without going outside the camp in bad weather. Ernest said he didn't have many problems. He said if you treat people right most of the time, they'll treat you right.

Ernest said he had some good people working there. Ray Wright, James Lupton, Edmond Gallop and, in the winter, Eddie Wheatley as a marsh guard.

In 1974 and '75, Mr. Slick built three cottages on Pine Island. He built one up on a high hill for himself from which you could see the sound and the ocean at the time. Trees may have grown up now so you can't. Then he built two more out east of the clubhouse but west of the road. One was for his daughter, Phyllis Cowell, and one for his attorney, Paul Micky.

Ernest Brickhouse and Mr. Slick's dog, Cindy. Ernest said the first thing Mr. Slick would do when he got to Pine Island was go to Cindy's pen, unlatch the gate and turn her out. She would follow him every step as long as he stayed there. When he got ready to go up and take a nap, she would follow him and lie on the floor right beside his bed. *Courtesy Ernest Brickhouse.*

Mr. Slick's grandchildren, Lynn and John Cowell, at Pine Island. *Courtesy Ernest Brickhouse.*

Ernest and Laverne Brickhouse's grandson, John Patton, and a Canada goose they named "Old Speck" because he had little white specks all the way down his neck. He went to Pine Island for twenty years. Then one year he didn't come, and they have never seen him since. He may have been shot on his way down from Canada, or he may have died of natural causes. We'll never know. That's life. *Courtesy Ernest Brickhouse.*

Mr. Donald O'Brien, *left*, chairman of the board of the National Audubon Society, and Ernest Brickhouse. *Courtesy Ernest Brickhouse.*

Deer and pintails at Pine Island. *Courtesy Ernest Brickhouse.*

Ernest said they spent right much time here in the summer. He said sometimes they'd go fishing and sometimes they'd go out to the beach. He said he always sent somebody with them to look out for the kids in case they wanted to get in the ocean.

I asked Ernest his impression of Mr. Earl Slick. He said, "He was one of a kind. He was a very conservative-minded person. Everything he did here he wanted to make Currituck County better. He was very considerate and did a lot of things that nobody knew about. Whatever he did he wanted to do and not make a big to-do about it."

Foreman

Roberts Brothers' Float Rig

John Wood Foreman was from Elizabeth City, North Carolina, and was in the lumber business. Foreman Blades Lumber Company owned a farm on the north end on Narrow Shore in Currituck County.

Lofton Riddick, hereafter referred to as "Preacher," moved his family to this farm in 1944 to look after the farm for Foreman.

Incidentally, this is the same farm that Abraham Baum bought when he sold the 3,100 acres on Currituck Beach to the men from New York who started Currituck Club for $3,100. Abraham Baum was my grandmother Carrie McHorney Boswood's granddaddy. He still had land and cattle on the beach. Granny told me she used to go across the sound with him in a sail canoe to take hay to his cattle.

Melvin and Celeus Roberts were prominent farmers in the Shawboro area of Currituck County. They had a big operation there by the railroad track on Gregory Road. In addition to their own farming operation, they sold seed, fertilizer, chemicals and more to other farmers. They bought and sold grain. They had a grain elevator, a dryer, a hardware store and an office in the store.

John Wood Foreman had Mr. Pat O'Neal build him a twenty-four-foot gas boat in 1947 with a concave tunnel in it so it would run in shallow water. It had a cabin with a windshield on it. The cabin was open in the back except for a roll-up

Foreman's dock at north end of Narrow Shore Road, Aydlett, North Carolina. This image shows the gas boat "Preacher" Riddick used to pull a float rig, 1966. *Courtesy Janet Riddick Sawyer.*

Foreman's boat, 1948. *Left to right*: Faye Jones, Bobby Miller, Elsie Jean Jackson and Kelly Miller. *Courtesy Janet Riddick Sawyer.*

John Wood, *left*, and Rodney Foreman in 1949 after a good day's hunt on Currituck Sound. *Courtesy Sophie F. Jordan.*

Above: John Wood Foreman's gas boat on a calm day in Currituck Sound; the men are changing in the float box. *Courtesy Sophie F. Jordan.*

Right: John Wood Foreman in 1995 at Nags Head, where he had one of the big old houses on the oceanfront with cedar shakes. I developed Aydlett Soundside for him, and he would stop by my office on his way from his home in Elizabeth City to the beach with his maid in the back seat. He'd want to know how things were going, and he'd say, "Just keep it in low forward." My first wife, Frances, was living then and in the business with me. She said John Wood knows how to live. He was one of the best people I ever worked with. *Courtesy Sophie F. Jordan.*

John Wood Foreman with his daughters, Sophie and Nancy, after a goose hunt on Currituck Sound. Sophie told me on her wedding day at the reception that Allen Foreman told her he just couldn't imagine John Wood Foreman's daughter getting married on the first day of bird season. *Courtesy Sophie F. Jordan.*

curtain. It had a seat on each side and a Chrysler Crown Marine engine. He also built him a twenty-foot skiff to take the decoys and float box he had him build.

Let me take time to tell you young people what a float box is. When they outlawed the old sink boxes, or "batteries" as they were locally called, Mr. Pat came up with this float box. The principle was the same as a sink box, although you were not below the water except for your feet. You were sitting level with the water, and your feet were below the water. It didn't have to have iron weights added, as the sink box did, because the weight of your body took care of the displacement for your feet below the water. It was legal because it didn't need artificial weight.

It had two wings in front, one on each side and one in the back. They were covered with burlap to cut the sea waves down. It had two runners under it that were as deep as the foot of the box. To transport it to the location you wanted to tie out, you would fold the wings up, and two good men could pull it across the washboards of the skiff. You usually had to cross tie it on the skiff if it was rough to keep it from sliding off the skiff.

Left to right: Allen Sawyer, Don Roberts and his daddy, Celeus Roberts, after a hunt in the float rig. *Courtesy Don Roberts.*

Preacher Riddick and Earl Baum tying out a float rig. Monkey Island is in background. *Courtesy Don Roberts.*

Vance Aydlett, *left*, and Lofton "Preacher" Riddick on top of the cabin of the Foreman boat. *Courtesy Janet Riddick Sawyer.*

In 1961, the Roberts brothers leased the farm from Foreman and put in a hog operation. At this time, they worked a deal with John Wood Foreman for them to use the hunting rig one day and then John Wood the next. Allen Sawyer worked in the hardware store, and he booked the days. Sometimes, John Wood would have a guest who wanted to go on a day that was for the Roberts brothers; if they had room, they'd take him and vice versa. This arrangement lasted until 1978, when Celeus's health started failing, and they got out of the hog business and divided up their farms.

Preacher Riddick ran the hunting rig for them. At various times, he had different people help him. The ones I know of are Earl Baum, Newton Hampton, Clyde "Booty" Spruill, Vance Aydlett and Levie Bunch Jr., not necessarily in that order, and I'm sure there were others.

They would go across the sound every day and usually take four hunters. They'd put two in what "Hambone" (Ambrose Twiford) called a dog box (box blind with no place to hide the skiff), which was on the south end of Green Lump Shoal, and usually tie the other two in the float box in Peters Quarter. They could wait on both rigs with the gas boat that way. They had other bush blinds, too, but that is the one he used most.

I hunted with my float rig many days in that same area, taking sportsmen or friends. I'd see Preacher crossing the sound in all kinds of weather with that rig. Foreman's boat just had a cabin and a windshield. My boat had what I called a shelter cabin in addition to the forward cabin, and I didn't get wet.

Don Roberts told me about one day when Preacher took him and his daddy (Celeus) and Allen Sawyer hunting. It was a cold, cloudy, blustery day. Don and Allen were in the box. Allen shot from his left shoulder with a twenty-gauge Browning automatic. It was about three o'clock in the afternoon, and they were sitting there about half asleep. Don heard geese,

Left to right: Jimmy Mason, Ron Jackson and Don Roberts after a duck hunt in the float rig. *Courtesy Don Roberts.*

A Roberts Brothers bush blind tied out in Currituck Sound. *Courtesy Don Roberts.*

and about the same time Allen punched him. He looked up, and seven geese had dropped down close to the water and had their wings set for the decoys. Preacher, Celeus and Earl were in the gas boat about five hundred yards away.

Preacher and Celeus were in the cabin half nodding, and Earl Baum was running the boat and looking at the geese through binoculars. Preacher said, "Are they going to 'em Earl?" Earl said, "Yea it looks like several are going in there to 'em." Pretty soon, Allen and Don both emptied their guns, and Preacher said, "Did they break anything down?" Celeus asked, "How many are left?" Earl said, "I ain't seen nothin' leave." Preacher said, "Earl you better hurry over there and get them out before they kill every duck in the sound."

Working with "Preacher" Riddick

As Told by Newton Hampton

Newton was helping Lofton "Preacher" Riddick with the float rig between 1962 and 1965. This story was told to me by Newton Hampton. He said it started out as an ordinary day. It was John Wood Foreman, Rodney Foreman, Beans Weatherly and Oop Ward. They loaded everything up and headed across the sound. They had been tying out in Peters Quarter and doing good there.

This day, they tied the outside blind on Green Lump Shoal and the float box in Peters Quarter. Later in the day, a real dark cloud started making up in the north. They decided they had better go take up the outside blind because they had to take up both rigs and didn't know how bad it was going to get. They took the decoys up and got the men out of the blind.

By the time they got back to the float rig, this black cloud was coming right down the beach. When it hit, it was blowing, snowing and freezing every drop that was flying, and the wind just kept right on picking up.

It was blowing so hard they couldn't pick up the decoys with the skiff. They were afraid they couldn't pole back to the gas boat. They had a coil of line in the boat they could have used to tie the skiff to the gas boat and let it back, but they were afraid the anchor on the gas boat wouldn't hold.

Newton said he always did the poling and Preacher did the stacking because he wanted them in there a certain way. He tied all his marsh ducks on one side and the diving ducks on the other, and they had to be taken up that way.

They decided that the only way they could take up was with the gas boat. They left the float blind in the water. By the time they got all the decoys in the stern of the boat, it was loaded in the stern.

Newton said there was no way they could go back across the sound. The wind was coming right straight down the sound blowing so hard it was blowing the tops off the waves and steady picking up. They would have had a beam sea, and everybody except Preacher agreed they just couldn't make it. Preacher thought they could. Newton said it was blowing harder and harder and getting colder and colder. The boat was just a sheet of ice, and it was getting dark on them.

They said, "What are we going to do?" Newton said, "We can go in the basin at the Whalehead Club." Atlantic Research owned the property at the time and was testing rocket fuel there then. Shirley and Gene Austin, who were natives of Currituck and the caretakers there, saw them coming and were standing on the dock when they got in. Shirley and Gene took them in at the Whalehead Club, and they called home and told their families they were all right.

Shirley fixed them supper and gave each of them a bedroom to sleep in. Gene called them up at daybreak the next morning, and Shirley had breakfast on the table when they got downstairs. It was a beautiful day but still cold. They got in the gas boat and went back to their rig. The skiff was iced up. They beat the ice off, bailed it out, pulled the box on and headed on back across the sound. The men from Elizabeth City went on home, and Newton and Preacher spent the rest of the day straightening up the decoys. They didn't go hunting the next day.

Newton said he'd never seen it get that bad that quick. He said he had some people tied for Casey Jones one time later on and saw a snowstorm come like that. He was tied north of Monkey Island in Henry Hampton's blind, but it never got bad enough he couldn't get the decoys up, get the two men in the boat and come on back across the sound.

Newton said that one time Preacher Riddick got sick and had to go to the hospital. Mr. Pat O'Neal worked in his place for a week or two. The first time they tied out, Mr. Pat was throwing ducks everywhere. Newton said, "Mr. Pat, we ought to tie all those canvasback over here and all the marsh ducks over there." Mr. Pat said, "Ah it don't make no difference; that's one of Riddick's things." Newton said when Preacher got back, the first time they tied out when they got ready to pick up they poled around and got all the canvasback and redheads, and then they picked up the marsh ducks and the geese. They got everything back just so, the way Preacher wanted it.

Miss Delie Spruill (Booty Spruill's mother) had a little restaurant about a half a mile south of Coinjock Bridge. Newton said she'd be in there early enough mornings that he'd stop by there on his way to Narrow Shore and go in the back door, and she'd have his breakfast ready for him. She charged him one dollar, and then he could go on and be at the dock about the same time the bunch from Elizabeth City got there. They didn't leave the landing until daylight or a little after.

Newton said the Foreman group and the Roberts group would most always bring eggs, ham, hamburgers or deer sausage, and Preacher would cook it on a little charcoal stove he kept in the middle of the cabin.

Rescue

Newton told me another time when he and Preacher had the float box tied in Peters Quarter, and somebody was in the blind on the shoal. They were just idling around as we always did, waiting on a float rig. We never anchored, just circled around; that kept the game stirred up, too.

They saw what looked like a rig tied out there in deep water. They thought that was funny because it was not there when they made the circle before. They started to go on by because the people in the rig were waving, and they thought they were waving for them to get away from them when, in fact, they were waving for them to come to them.

Newton kept looking, and he told Preacher that something was wrong—he couldn't see no blind or anything, so they turned around. When they got to them, it was Marvin Fulcher and his daddy, Willard. They were going across the sound in a skiff when it took a run on a sea, took a nose dive, run its bow under and sunk. What Newton and Preacher saw were decoys floating all over everywhere.

When Marvin and his daddy saw them turn away, they thought they were going to bypass them. Newton said when they got there that Mr. Willard was just about gone. They got Marvin in the boat, and it was all he, Newton and Preacher could do to get Mr. Willard in the boat. They took right off and carried them straight to the dock and then took them home.

Mr. Willard had a big gas boat, and as soon as they dried out and warmed up they were back out in the sound trying to gather up their rig. They lost their guns. They didn't have any life preservers. The bow of the skiff would float because it was wood. The stern was down because the motor was on it. Marvin said he had held his daddy up about as long as he could. If Preacher and Newton hadn't come along, they would soon have been gone.

Frank Midyette Carter

January 1, 1913-April 1, 1995

Frank Carter was born in Hyde County, Fairfield, North Carolina. In 1928, he moved to Coinjock to work for the Coast and Geodetic Survey. His brother, Charles, lived in Coinjock and worked with the survey, and he got Frank the job.

In 1937, he married a local girl, Elizabeth "Libby" Bray. They had three children: William, Suzann and Walton. Frank quit the survey in 1945.

In 1941, he had begun to take leave from his work during the hunting and fishing seasons. In 1945, he went to full-time hunting, fishing and shrimping. He guided hunting and fishing parties in Currituck Sound, Coinjock, Cedar Island Bays and North River.

In 1946, he moved to the canal bank in Coinjock, where he lived the rest of his life. He hunted stationary blinds until 1950, when he had Clarence O'Neal of Aydlett build him a float box. Bill Beasley of Coinjock built him a new hunting skiff big enough to carry the float box.

He made his decoys and patterned them after Ned Burgess decoys. When Ned Burgess died, he bought the patterns and the remaining uncarved heads and goose bodies from the family.

Mr. Frank stopped taking hunting parties in the 1980s but continued taking fishing parties until 1994. He worked with T. Ray Hassell in Chesapeake, Virginia, surveying for about thirty years.

Frank Midyette Carter. *Courtesy Walton Carter.*

When my Daddy, Chester Morris, died on December 20, 1972, Mr. Frank knew I was carrying sportsmen. He sent his son, Walton, to see me and tell me that if I had men to carry hunting he'd take them for me and wouldn't charge me anything. I really appreciated that. That's the way it used to be around here. People would help one another. When I was farming, if a neighbor got behind and the grass was about to take his crop or he couldn't get it harvested, a neighbor would bring his tractor or combine and help him.

Next I'm going to let Wayne Twiford tell you about working with Mr. Frank Carter.

Frank Carter

As Told by Wayne Penn Twiford

Wayne Twiford graduated from high school in 1956. He said Mr. Frank Carter had always been a friend of his family, and that fall Frank asked him if he'd run one of his float box rigs for him. He had two gas boats. One was an old boat about thirty feet long. It had a cabin but no shelter cabin or canopy to stand under when you were running it. He had this boat a long time and used it to fish a haul seine net. He also had a big old thirty-three-foot shad boat they called the *Gray Goose*. He bought it from somebody up in Great Bridge, Virginia. This boat had a lot of history. The boat was built in 1906 in Wanchese by Otis Doe. I'll tell more about this boat in a later chapter.

Wayne was going to run the old boat that Mr. Frank used. Wayne said he'd never forget how Mr. Frank called him just before bedtime the night before he was to make his first trip and told him that the wind was going to shift to the northwest. Now remember, we didn't have good weather reporting like we have now. He went by the glass (barometer) and by the way things looked. He said, "It's going to shift tomorrow afternoon, probably before taking up time; I'm just not sure, but why don't you take your rig over there on the southeast side of the Gull Rock. There are some ducks and geese over there, and you'll be in the lee of that shoal if it hits before you take up." He said to look for it to blow. "It may not last long, but when it hits it's gonna blow."

Frank Carter and Linwood Fulcher tying out a float rig. Sportsmen are in the float box. *Courtesy Walton Carter.*

Frank Carter's float rig tied out in Currituck Sound. *Courtesy Walton Carter.*

Wayne said he did what Mr. Frank told him to do. When he tied out, it was just as pretty a day as you could ask for. About 1:00 p.m., he began to see some clouds up in the northwest. About 1:30 p.m., the wind shifted and it blew. He said he was glad he was in the lee of that shoal.

Wayne said he was really impressed. He said he thought to himself, "This is somebody I better listen to." I asked Wayne who had helped him. He said part of the time Guy Parker and part of the time Julian Curles. The days Mr. Frank didn't have enough men for two rigs, Wayne would get on the boat with Mr. Frank and help him. The *Gray Goose* had a big cabin on it, and Mr. Frank had a stove in there. Wayne said along about ten o'clock Mr. Frank would say, "What'a you want for dinner?" Wayne said, "I don't care." Mr. Frank said, "Well, I'd like to have some blue peters."

He'd give Wayne a handful of shells and put him in a blind or on a point of marsh, and he'd run a bunch of blue peters by him, and Wayne would kill some. Then he'd get back on the boat, skin them out and wash them right overboard. He said he would put some grease in a little frying pan they had, flour the blue peters and fry 'em. Then he put flour in the grease that was left and made gravy. Then they'd take loaf bread and sop up the gravy. "Didn't

Mr. Frank Carter mending a net in a fishing skiff at Casey Jones dock in Waterlily. *Courtesy Walton Carter.*

Frank Carter, *left*, guiding Hugh Murray III while bass fishing. They're coming out of Cedar Island Bay. *Courtesy Walton Carter.*

have no plates or nothin'; just a piece of newspaper or somethin' to lay the blue peters on." Wayne said just about every day Mr. Frank would want blue peters. He said he got so tired of blue peters he didn't know what to do. After cooking all those blue peters, he called him Wayne "Peter" Twiford.

Wayne said he commercial fished with him a couple of years, and then he carried some bass fishermen for him who stayed with Miss Elsie Carter, Mr. Frank's sister-in-law.

Wayne said another thing that Mr. Frank taught him was that early in a morning, when day was just breaking and before the sun comes up, if you look out across the sound to the east and it looks like a "gum swamp," as Mr. Frank called it, he said, "You can look out; it's gonna blow."

Mr. Casey Jones told me the same thing, except he called it a "high bank." The higher that bank of clouds, the harder it's gonna blow. Some mornings, I'd be leaving the dock, and Mr. Casey would say, "Boy, you'd better put her behind a shoal today; it's gonna blow." I took his advice and still keep that in mind today regardless of what the weatherman says.

Mr. Frank told Wayne that he needed to get out and get a real job. He got a job on a tugboat. He worked twenty days on and ten days off. On his off days, he still hunted and fished with Mr. Frank for many years.

Wayne made a career out of tugboating. He worked his way up to captain and did that until he retired. His wife, June, was the first cook we had when we started Piney Island Club in 1983. Wayne was still tugboating then.

Wayne said one time that he and his daddy, Roland Twiford, were fishing with Mr. Frank, and they were going to make a haul off Knapp's pier in front of Mackey Island. On the way up there, they were going across the edge of Great Shoal. Mr. Frank and Roland were talking about one time in World War II when a plane went down out there. They said a big engine fell off it before it hit the water. The propeller fell off and stuck in the bottom, and it was sticking straight up; then, after a few days, it kept leaning over until you couldn't see it anymore. Mr. Frank started looking around and said, "You know what, that old engine is somewhere right along here." He hadn't more than gotten it out of his mouth when they hit something and knocked a hole in the boat, and water was just gushing in. He turned it for the highest part of the shoal, and it sunk right out from under them. Of course they had the big fishing skiff in tow. They got in that. The wind was blowing a right good breeze from the northeast, which pushed them on toward the north end of Churches Island. They picked up a couple of the spuds and helped it along. When they got ashore, they got a ride down the island to Grissie Barco's. They got him, several pumps, a bunch of rags and Mr. Frank's other gas boat and went back up there. They got it pumped up enough they could roll it over to one side, enough so Grissie could get a patch on it and get it back to the island and onto Grissie's railway. It didn't hurt the engine.

Wayne said that when he was hunting for Mr. Frank, the deal was he would get fifteen dollars per day for the days he hunted, but every week at the end of the week when he got paid Mr. Frank always gave him more than he bargained for. Wayne Twiford thought a lot of Frank Carter, and apparently it was mutual respect.

I'll tell a couple of short stories about times I took sportsmen for Mr. Frank. He called me up one night and asked me if I'd take two sportsmen for him the next day. He wasn't feeling good. He may have had a bad cold or something.

I was to meet them at the Walnut Island Motel the next morning. At the time, I had my rig at Charlie Dozier's landing in Jarvisburg. There were some ducks down there in Dews Quarter Bay, and I'd moved my rig down there.

When we got ready to get in the boat, they had a bottle of whiskey. I told them they couldn't take that on my boat. I didn't care how much they drank when they got ashore, but I didn't think gunpowder and whiskey mixed. I told them if they didn't want to go that was all right. They said that was okay. What I didn't know was they had flasks in their pockets.

Fred Newbern was helping me that day. We had the one-man lay down box, so they would have to take turns getting in it. It was a really cold, overcast day. We got it tied out. The sportsmen we had were Hugh Murray III and his friend, Ed Meadows, who played for the Chicago Bears. Hugh Murray got in the box first. We went off in the gas boat to stir up a little game. It wasn't long before we heard one shot. Then he was standing up, waving his arms. I chugged on along up to the rig, and he was standing up in the middle of the box, and it was full of water. It didn't sink because it was all wood. What happened was his gun went off accidentally and shot a hole in the box. He was very lucky he didn't shoot his foot off. Needless to say, that ended that hunt.

Another time, I was taking two men for Mr. Frank and still had my rig at Charlie Dozier's landing in Jarvisburg. This time I was using the two-man sit up box.

I met with the men the night before at Miss Elsie Carter's, where they were staying. One was an old man who was a retired general in the army. The other man was young, and they had come up from South Carolina on his plane. I think he was in the business of selling and financing house trailers. I had been out in the sound the day before, and Dews Quarter bay was full of ducks. I was telling them about all the ducks and really getting their adrenaline pumping.

The next morning, we went out there in Dews Quarter Bay, and there was not a duck to be seen anywhere. It made me feel like a fool. The general was so old and clumsy I really needed a boom and block and tackle to get him in the box.

There were no ducks. We didn't even see a duck. I finally managed to swim a bunch of geese to them, and they got their geese. That night I went home, got some ducks out of our freezer and gave them to them so they would have ducks to take home.

That trip taught me a lesson I still respect to this day: Never tell anybody how many ducks you see, because they may be just passing through and gone tomorrow.

Decoys

Mr. Frank Carter made all his decoys, so his son Walton told me. He said he'd get blocks of juniper from over at Mose White's at Morgan's Corner, bring them home and chop them into quarters. He'd shape the duck up and then make a head. He patterned his decoys after Ned Burgess decoys.

Walton said his daddy taught Ambrose Twiford, "Hambone," how to make decoys. Hambone would come around and watch Mr. Frank. He started making the head by making the bill first. Mr. Frank told him to leave the bill until last. What he had looked like a cigar. If you will notice, the bills on Hambone's decoys are all wide now.

One time, I heard somebody ask Hambone how to make a decoy. He said get you a block of wood and chop away everything that don't look like a duck to you. I thought that was a pretty good answer.

Coast Guard License

I need to tell you how this Coast Guard license (pictured on the next page) came about. I had one just like it until my office burned down in 1980.

In 1957, Henry Doxey was running an old thirty-two-foot battery boat (so called because it was used to haul a battery or sink box when they were legal) for Charlie Snowden. He would leave Mill Landing at Maple with five to seven skiffs in tow and have a guide for each rig, with two sportsmen and a guide for each skiff on board.

He would tow them across Coinjock Bay, through the haul over out past Goose Castle, to Great Shoal in the middle of Currituck Sound, where he would drop the rigs off to bush blinds. The guides didn't have outboard motors, just shoving poles. If a guide went out to pick up a dead duck and couldn't get back, Henry would see him and come tow him back to his blind.

One day, a strong northeaster came up quick—so quick they had to leave their rigs. Henry picked up the guides and men. He also picked up other people who were in trouble. By this time, the old boat was really loaded, and when they were going around Goose Castle it was taking on a lot of water, and the guides were taking turns pumping. There were no electric bilge pumps then. Some of the men wanted to know where the life jackets were. Henry told them there weren't any. When they got in, somebody

SERIAL NUMBER A94629

ISSUE NUMBER -1-

UNITED STATES COAST GUARD

LICENSE

TO OPERATE OR NAVIGATE MOTORBOATS CARRYING PASSENGERS FOR HIRE

This is to certify that FRANK MIDGETTE CARTER *has given satisfactory evidence to the undersigned, that he can safely be intrusted with the duties and responsibilities of operator of motorboats as defined in the Act of April 25, 1940, when carrying passengers for hire on the navigable waters of* *** ~~the United States~~ *and is hereby licensed to act as such operator for the term of five years from this date.*

** *Given under my hand this* 6th *day of* NOVEMBER, *19* 57

***CURRITUCK SOUND, NORTH RIVER AND CONTIGUOUS NORTHERN WATERS DURING THE HOURS OF DAYLIGHT ONLY FOR CLASS A AND CLASS "1" AND "2" MOTORBOATS.

NORFOLK, VIRGINIA — *Port*

Officer in Charge, Marine Inspection

Coast Guard license. *Courtesy Walton Carter.*

reported it to the Coast Guard. To make a long story short, all the guides who were taking sportsmen for hire in Currituck had to go to Griggs School in Poplar Branch; a Coast Guardsman came down there and gave us a test and licenses like the one shown here.

History of the Gray Goose former Red Wing

As Told by Jarvis Snow

You have to remember that this story takes place in the Depression of the late '20s and early '30s. At that time, people were losing their homes and farms. It was just hard to make a dollar, and people did anything they could to survive.

Mr. Dexter Snow lived at Powells Point in Currituck County. He and his wife, Belinda, had two sons and a daughter. Julian was the oldest and then daughter Murden and then Jarvis. They had a farm that they were about to lose.

Mr. Dexter and his brother, Marchant, each had thirty-three-foot shad boats. They were built by Otis Doe in Wanchese. The one Mr. Dexter had was built in 1906. It had a Red Wing engine in it when he got it, thus the name *Red Wing*, although he soon took that out and put a Palmer Marine engine in it.

Mr. Dexter and Marchant started working for a man named Speed Fentress, who lived in the Virginia Beach area of Virginia. They were hauling liquor from a still on Mill Tail Creek in East Lake across Albemarle Sound and up Currituck Sound to Gallop's Landing in Powells Point. Jarvis told me the still was so big it would blow a steam whistle for the men to knock off and go back to work at lunch. There was nobody around except the ones working at the still.

Gray Goose (former *Red Wing*) built by Otis Doe in Wanchese in 1906. It was rebuilt by Walton Carter in 1978, and he had Bruce Bess cover it with fiberglass at that time. This picture was taken at the Wright Brothers landing in Jarvisburg on November 6, 2009. The boat now belongs to Jerry Wright. He bought it to preserve so it could be displayed in the boathouse at the Whalehead Club. *Author's collection.*

Jarvis said the *Red Wing* would haul 104 five-gallon jugs of liquor. He said the liquor was so potent you could spill some on the ground and stick a match to it and it would burn a blue flame. His daddy told him that liquor was for selling, not drinking. His daddy also told him when he got the mortgage paid off the farm that he was through hauling it.

Jarvis said when they loaded it that they would put burlap bags between the jugs to keep them from breaking. Then they would cover it all with a canvas and tack it to the washboards to keep the spray out.

When they got to Gallop's Landing, most of the time cars would be there to get it. He said the folks who were hauling it were from Virginia and hauling it there. They were driving Pierce Arrows and souped-up Buicks, and one had a Cadillac. Each driver loaded the liquor the way he wanted it. They would back the cars down to the water's edge. It was hard bottom. There was a little soft place ahead of it, and if they got stuck another one would pull him out.

If you've seen a five-gallon jug you know it has a finger hole right in the neck. Jarvis said if there were no cars there when they came in, they would put the liquor overboard and run a line through those finger holes to tie them together. When the cars came, they would take a drag and pick up the line.

Jarvis said the *Red Wing* had two sixty-gallon gas tanks, one on each side. He said Mr. Osborn Hampton, who was the Standard Oil dealer in Coinjock, would send his oil truck to Gallop's Landing to fill the boats up. He said they would haul sugar back to East Lake, so they were loaded both ways.

The boat Marchant was running caught fire in the Albemarle Sound in 1931, and he lost his life. Jarvis said they found him in a fishnet. He had a cork life jacket and rain gear on. He said when they found him, blood was running down his face where the cork jacket and snaps on his rain gear had beat up against him. Apparently, he had just died because the blood was still running.

There was another man with him whose name Jarvis thought was Abraham Gallop. Apparently he lost his life at the scene.

Jarvis said that sometimes his daddy would have to take the liquor on to Mundon's Point at the North Carolina/Virginia line. Once in a while, he would have to take it on to Norfolk. When he went through the locks at Great Bridge, they would want to know what he had on, and he'd tell them fish. He didn't like to do that because that was real risky, even though it was covered with canvas.

Mr. Dexter had another smaller boat that Jarvis's older brother Julian ran. It would only hold forty jugs of liquor but was faster. It had a Pierce Arrow engine out of a car in it. He said it had double ignition with two spark plugs for each cylinder. You could cut it on using one or both. If you put it on both it'd really take off.

He said one time the officers were expecting them. When they got to Coinjock Bridge, the bridge was up (the bridge raised up instead of swung around). He put it in reverse and turned around right quick. When he did, I think it was Bryan Bright who was a deputy sheriff and shot right through the door of the car. Lucky it didn't hit the driver. He high-tailed it back to Powells Point, and Jarvis said he hid the liquor in a hotbed out back of the house. When the law got there, of course, the car was empty. The next day, Speed Fentress called and wanted to know why the liquor didn't get there. His daddy told him what happened. Speed said he'd be right down there. Jarvis said he came down in a big Pierce Arrow with a 30-30 on the front seat. He said, "Let them try to shoot me." They loaded him up and he went to Virginia.

Jarvis said one time, when he was just a little boy, he was trying to take two five-gallon jugs up the dock. He had to twist to get between two of the posts on the dock, and the jugs banged together and busted. He said he knew

Dexter Snow, 1943. When Ray Adams leased the Whalehead Club to the Coast Guard it was with the provisions that Dexter Snow be made a chief boatswain's mate; his son, Julian, be made a first class boatswain's mate; and they be stationed at the Whalehead Club to look after Mr. Adams's interest. *Courtesy Jarvis Snow.*

Dexter Snow, Ray Adams and Dexter Snow's son Julian (closing barn door) at Dexter's house in Powells Point. *Courtesy Jarvis Snow.*

An image of Erleen and Jarvis Snow, taken at the foot of the Currituck Sound Bridge with 1937 and 1938 Fords. Note the fog lights, spotlight and side mirrors. Jarvis always had his cars dressed up and shined up. Erleen delivered the newspaper when I was young, and I was impressed by how shiny her car always was. *Courtesy Jarvis Snow.*

his daddy was going to get on him for that because those five-gallon jugs of liquor were worth forty dollars apiece, but he didn't.

Jarvis said one time he and Julian had gone to East Lake to get a load by car. When they got back to the Manns Harbor ferry, Julian knew the captain. The captain asked him if he had anything in the car. Julian told him yes. The captain told him they were checking all the cars on the other side. Julian asked him if he could hold the ferry fifteen minutes. He said he could. Jarvis said they turned around and went back to somebody's house they knew who would let them leave the liquor there and unloaded it. They went back to the ferry and went on across. Sure enough, the revenuers were there and checked them. Of course they were clean, but if it hadn't been for the captain they would have been caught.

When this was all over, Mr. Dexter Snow became superintendent of Whalehead Club from 1941 (the year after Mr. Ray Adams bought it) until Mr. Adams died in 1959. When Mr. Adams leased the Whalehead property to the Coast Guard during World War II, some of the conditions were that Dexter Snow be made a chief boatswain's mate and his son Julian be made a first class boatswain's mate and that they be stationed at the Whalehead Club to look after Mr. Adams's interest.

Ray Adams with a Load of Game

Here is Ray Adams with a trunk-load of game to take back to Washington, D.C. Jarvis Snow said that this was the way he carried the ducks back to Washington until one day when the federal game warden, Albert Sumrell, was stopping everybody at the state line.

For those of you who read this and don't know who Ray Adams was, he was in the meatpacking business in Washington, D.C., and sold a lot of meat to the Coast Guard; he also owned the Whalehead Club.

Ray Adams with a trunk-load of game. *Courtesy Jarvis Snow.*

He bought the Whalehead Club with all furnishings and four and a half miles of beach from the Atlantic Ocean to Currituck Sound from the estate of Edward Collins Knight Jr. He paid $25,000 for it, with a $2,500 down payment; the balance over nine years would hold at 4 percent interest.

On August 20, 1940, Mr. Herbert O. Frey, vice-president of the Pennsylvania Company, executors of the Knight estate, wrote to Mr. Adams, telling him that their trust committee had approved his offer. My Daddy, Chester Morris, was Mr. Adams's attorney, and I had this letter in my office until it burned down in 1980.

Erleen Snow

Famous Goose-Calling Champ

Erleen Gallop Snow and her husband, Jarvis, are shown here at the Currituck Wildlife Show. She was three times the state voice goose-calling champion. In 1988, she attracted thirteen thousand people to the Smithsonian Institution, where her performance was recorded to become part of the permanent archives.

She was also on the *Today Show*. Jarvis said that every time she was on television the number of strangers stopping by their house increased.

Erleen Gallop Snow and her husband Jarvis at the Currituck Wildlife Show. *Courtesy Jarvis Snow.*

Jimmy Markert brought two or three Canada geese we had at Piney Island (whose wings were clipped at the time) to the Currituck Wildlife Show. People would walk by the pen and honk at them, and the geese would just look at them. Erleen would talk to them and they'd talk back to her. She said that she learned to call geese from her daddy, Ervin Gallop. He was at Currituck Club.

She was the only woman to ever honk her way to a national championship.

Walton Carter and Billy Brumsey

Episode on the Gray Goose

Billy and Walton went hunting one morning. It was a pretty slick, calm day, so they didn't hunt too long. They decided to take the boat and go boat riding.

They were about in the middle of Currituck Sound when Carter told Brumsey to check the gas can to see how much was in it. Brumsey picked up hard on it like it was full, but it was empty. He picked up so hard on it he liked to have thrown it overboard. Carter said, "Well we've got to go in to Corolla and get five gallons." (Speaking of gas cans, Carter had a three-gallon gas can with a door made in the bottom in case he had over-the-limit of ducks—he could put them in that can. That can is on display in the North Carolina Wildlife Resources Museum in Corolla now.)

After they got the gas, they ran on down toward Poplar Branch and ran into Allen Foreman. Allen had a rig tied out and had to use the bathroom but didn't have any toilet paper. Carter always kept some on the boat, so he threw him a roll. Soon Allen left, and when Carter went to start the boat up and put it in gear he heard *thump*, and the motor choked down. He looked back, and the towline to the skiff was in the wheel. Brumsey said, "What are we going to do now?" Carter had taken a Stillson wrench and tried to turn the wheel backward, and it wouldn't turn. Carter said, "Well, one of us has got to go overboard." He said they were pretty well in their cups by

Gray Goose is the last boat out on the right at Jones dock in Waterlily, 1975. *Author's collection.*

then, anyway. He was still working with the shaft when he heard *kabloop*. Carter looked up and Brumsey had gone overboard. He came up blowing like a whale with milfoil all over him. When he finally got his breath, he said, "Carter what do I do now?" Carter said, "You go underneath the boat and get the rope off." Brumsey went under the boat and finally got it off and got back in the boat. He was about to freeze. That water was cold. He got his clothes back on. They had a drink or two and kept on going.

When Walton Carter, Billy Brumsey and Tommy Moore were all divorced, the *Gray Goose* was involved in a lot of episodes that I know about that can't be printed here.

Gray Goose at Monkey Island

When I was running Monkey Island in the '70s, I invited to the island Baxter Williams, who was a close friend of mine and chairman of the Currituck County Board of Commissioners; Billy Brumsey, county attorney; Graham Pervier, county manger; and Walton Carter, who worked under Graham as head of the Planning and Inspection

Department. I was chairman of the Planning Board. I invited all of them over to Monkey Island to go duck hunting.

They came over to the island the afternoon before in the *Gray Goose*. Shirley Austin, who was cooking there at the time, had a big supper for us.

I said this in one of my other books when Shirley was alive, but I want to say it again. Shirley Austin was an excellent cook. She lived in Corolla when there were no roads there, and she could drive the beach with the best of them. She had her real estate license with me and worked in my office, and she came five miles across Currituck Sound by herself in a boat every day to the office. She could also type and keep books. She and her husband, Gene, had a room at the club during the hunting season. She cooked and he guided.

Back to the story. We always kept a roaring oak fire in the clubroom. After supper, we were sitting around the fire watching a little television and spinning yarns. Between the drinks, the steamed oysters before supper, the big meal Shirley prepared for us and the roaring oak fire, we were falling asleep, so we all got up and went to bed.

We were up at five o'clock the next morning, and Shirley had a big breakfast of eggs, country ham, biscuits, red eye gravy and hot coffee.

Monkey Island Club, 1970s. *Author's collection.*

Billy Brumsey on the *Gray Goose*. *Author's collection.*

Walton Carter, Billy Brumsey and Baxter Williams at Monkey Island. *Author's collection.*

When we went out it was nineteen degrees. I can't remember what Baxter and I did; we may have stayed in by the fire. Carter, Graham and Billy took the *Gray Goose* and a skiff with decoys and went down to Mary Island.

He was going to put Graham in a blind on the north end of the island. When Graham was getting out of the boat on the marsh, he wouldn't wait for Carter to get up there close enough, and he fell in a muskrat hole and went over his boots. Graham said, "Boys I'm going to freeze to death."

Carter said, "Ah don't worry about it. When the sun comes up pull your socks off and hang them on the blind and let them dry out."

Carter and Brumsey went on down to another blind about midway of the island. Where spray had gotten on his gun and frozen, Carter said he had to stick his finger in his gun barrel to warm it up so he could get a shell in there.

Brumsey and Carter killed a few ducks, and they'd hear Graham shoot once in a while, so they knew he was still alive.

After the sun came up in a little while, they decided they'd better go check on him. When they came up to the blind, his socks were hanging on it. He came out of the blind with a sweater on one foot and a glove on the other. He said, "Boys I know how they felt at Valley Forge now." They came on back to the clubhouse and thawed out. We probably went back out hunting later in the day.

Leon A. Dunn Jr.

I'm going to close this book with a tribute to a charter member of Piney Island Club and a close friend of mine, Lindy Dunn. After a hard fight with cancer, he passed on to be with his Maker on July 10, 2009.

Lindy was not that much of a hunter and therefore was not included in many of the stories in my previous books about DeWitt McCotter, Sandy Thorpe and me, but I want him to be remembered.

Lindy loved boats and I love boats. When he got in the club, he had a forty-plus-foot sailboat, *Peppermint Pattie.* In 1985, my oldest daughter, Ruth, was just getting her hair back from chemo after a long battle with cancer. Ruth loves boats, too. Her mother, Frances, and I were going to take her down the Intracoastal Waterway (ICW) to Fort Lauderdale, Florida, in an old forty-foot wood Owens motor yacht I had. Herbert and Iva Lange were going with us. Herbert is a retired master chief engineman in the Coast Guard. We became close friends in 1951 when I got in the Coast Guard and have been ever since. I didn't take any long trips on the boat without him.

Lindy heard me talk about this trip and heard me say that Frances and Ruth were going to fly back from Fort Lauderdale. He had never made that trip up the ICW from Florida and wanted to know if he could come back with me. I told him since he was a sailboater and used to going slow (my boat cruises at twelve miles per hour) that he could come. I said if it was John

Frances M leaving Beach Marine in Jacksonville Beach, Florida, heading north. Lindy Dunn had just thrown off the lines and was climbing back up on the bridge, October 1985. *Author's collection.*

High I wouldn't let him come, because he couldn't stand to go that slow and would drive me nuts.

Lindy paid me back for that trip many times. Over the years, he bought three nice motor yachts and rode me many miles on them, as well as in his plane.

Lindy Dunn, DeWitt McCotter, Sandy Thorpe and I have been very close friends since 1983. They travel in a different world from me, but you wouldn't know that when we're together. They have always treated me as an equal. I'm just a poor country real estate broker who has had a single-wide trailer for an office since 1970. I have farmed, driven a truck, guided duck hunters and commercial fished to stay in Currituck. I have enjoyed my life, and I'm not intimidated by anyone.

When I turned seventy, Sandy, Lindy and DeWitt gave me a birthday party at Sandy's cabin in Rocky Mount, North Carolina. When I turned seventy-five, they had a party for me at Lindy's house on Bogue Sound in Morehead City, North Carolina. Lindy also has houses in Rocky Mount,

North Carolina, and Haig Point on Daufuskie Island, South Carolina. Dunn, McCotter and Thorpe all got out of Piney Island Club several years ago, but we stay in touch and get together every now and then. It may be in Florida, Rocky Mount or Currituck. I stayed in touch with Lindy Dunn as long as he lived, and he always ended the conversation with "Stay in touch."

I cannot improve on the eulogy that Lindy's son-in-law, Vince Andracchio II, gave at his funeral, and with quoting that I end this book:

> *Lindy Dunn was a great friend, a caring employer, civic leader and a devoted family man. Lindy loved his family. When I make that statement I speak not just of Pattie, Janie Mac, Genie and grandchildren—I mean his whole family. With Lindy a lot of people were family. His friends, his co-workers, his partners were all family. I have never known a person as inclusive as Lindy Dunn. He loved connecting with people and inquiring of people. He took the time to get to know you and because of this you knew*

My seventieth birthday party at Sandy Thorpe's cabin in Rocky Mount, North Carolina. *Left to right*: Sandy Thorpe, Jo Ann Morris, myself and Pattie Dunn; across from Pattie, *left to right*, is Brenda Thorpe, Lindy Dunn, Denny McCotter and DeWitt McCotter. *Author's collection.*

Lindy Dunn and Sandy Thorpe at Sandy's cabin. Dunn is telling me and McCotter a story. *Author's collection.*

My seventy-fifth birthday party at Lindy and Pattie Dunn's house in Morehead City, North Carolina. DeWitt McCotter and Lindy Dunn. *Author's collection.*

At Jo Ann Morris's cottage in Corolla, North Carolina. DeWitt McCotter, myself, Lindy Dunn and Sandy Thorpe. *Author's collection.*

he cared. When Lindy asked, "How are you," it was never perfunctory, he really wanted to know. As a result he bonded easily with friends from all geographies and all walks. One day he heard from a retired Federal Reserve president and from a baggage handler at Haig Point. The two calls were equally important to Lindy.

Now from that please don't think he was a pushover or softie. Lindy was a Marine and Lindy was his own man. He did not like being told what to do. Many of you know of Lindy's heart problems and all of you know about the leukemia he fought—but you may not know about his eye problems. His eyesight was deteriorating and he needed to have an eye surgery but couldn't while he battled leukemia. His eyesight got worse and worse until last fall, it became such a problem that one evening after a family get together, Janie Mac suggested I needed to tell him he needed to quit driving. The driving was a real problem and I took the suggestion seriously but I said, "When the time comes when I have to tell my father he has to quit driving, I will, but you are on your own with your father."

And Janie Mac came right back and rightfully said, "Well if we don't do something he's going to kill somebody." And to that I said, "But if I tell him to quit driving he'll kill me!" He never liked being told what to do.

Lindy had a wonderful sense of humor and his disease didn't change this. His laugh was described by a dear friend as "the best giggle east of the Mississippi." He loved throwing a zinger at you but you could always tell when it was coming. He'd get a twinkle in his eye and the corners of his mouth would turn up slightly to form a wry smile and then out it came. It happened on June 30—the last day of his last full month. Several friends were sitting with him on his back porch. Out of the blue, he looked up and said, "I need to make it until at least midnight tonight. Because if I don't we'll have to return the Social Security check for July!" And we heard the best giggle east of the Mississippi. A few days later when nurse Ratchet showed up to give him his medicine for the umpteenth time, he seemed asleep. She said, "Lindy, it's time for your medicine." Without opening his eyes, he said in a robotic voice, "This is a recording." And there was the smile.

Leukemia did not diminish Lindy's sense of humor and his bad eyesight never robbed him of the vision that carried him through life.

There is a saying that "an old man who cannot bid farewell to life appears as feeble and sickly as a young man who is unable to embrace it." Lindy suffered neither of these shortcomings. His final days were lived with dignity, grace and poise, reserved for only those ready for what lay ahead. And Lindy always embraced life…he really *embraced life. There was no hand he didn't play; there was no experience he didn't chase. One of his friends often says "Life is no dress rehearsal." I heard Lindy repeat this more than once, but more important, he lived it. At various times, he was in the ambulance business, the armored car business, the nursing home business, and campgrounds. He developed land, built houses, built restaurants and chased dreams. He thought his Uncle Charlie was crazy when he invested in a car wash and thought we were brilliant when we bought radio stations. As it relates to healthy food, he was indiscriminate. At one time he sold fried hamburgers and fried doughnuts. His next move was all organic with whole grain granola.*

Lindy was acquisitive. To my knowledge, he bought, built, and sold some 20 businesses. Houses were no exception—there were at least ten of those. He loved his boats and was in and out of them with the whims of the wind. He loved his airplanes. All of this came and went without attachment, without looking back.

In the final analysis, Lindy only had one true love and that's Pattie. While businesses, houses, boats, and planes came and went, Pattie was always with him. The marriage started in 1963, but the love affair started long before. Their love was the constant. Never did it vary. Never did it wane. Together the two of them built a family and, of all the things Lindy built, it was his family that gave him his pride and joy. He was a devoted husband to Pattie and a fabulous parent to Genie and Janie Mac. He never made any important decision without first considering its impact on the three of them.

If you spent time with Lindy you knew he grew up in Ayden, North Carolina. He never forgot his roots, or the lessons he learned growing up in a small town where kids could be kids and high school athletics ruled. When he came to Rocky Mount in 1966, he quickly became involved in the community. He worked with others in the 70s to save North Carolina Wesleyan College from imminent collapse. He later was involved in a laundry list of community endeavors—ranging from Scouting to the United Way. He was Senior Warden here at St. Andrews. Lindy always offered his time for the greater good. He's passed his beliefs about community and his attitude of participation on to Janie Mac and Genie and also to his grandchildren. This is a gift he's given them and a gift he's given to their respective communities.

His community mindedness must have started in Ayden. To hear Lindy talk of Ayden is to tell of Mayberry. His memories and tales of growing up in Ayden truly were enchanting. He had stories and sayings that would go on forever and he loved telling them. I know—because I heard every one of them—at least ten times. I called them Aydenisms. He and I had a standing rule that if I had heard a story more than 3 times, I'd raise my hand and he'd quit telling the story. There were sayings such as "tougher than wet goat hair" and there were stories about his dog Pal and the enema. These stories could fill a book and I know all of them by heart. I could share them here today, but just like movies, Aydenisms come with ratings. And there aren't many G-rated Aydenisms.

In his 20s Lindy was a hard charging Marine, in his 30s and 40s he was a hard charging entrepreneur. In his 50s he was a team builder and in his 60s he became the world's best cheerleader. Lindy turned 70 last October amidst his battle with leukemia. It may have been the wisdom gathered over the years or may have been the wisdom knowing death is eminent, but in his 70s he was a great adviser. He played all of these roles incredibly well without ever prioritizing any of them ahead of his family.

On only rare occasions are we brought together to give thanks for a life so well lived.

Lindy was an incredible parent, a loyal friend, a fair boss and inspiring leader. Today we celebrate this remarkable life.

Someone once said, "God pours life into death and death into life without a drop being spilled." As we say goodbye to our friend, we are thankful—that not a drop was spilled.

About the Author

Travis Morris was born in Coinjock, North Carolina, in 1932 (in the same house his mother was born in on April 3, 1908). He was the only child of Chester and Edna Morris. His daddy was an attorney and later a Superior Court judge. He represented many of the old duck hunting clubs when he was practicing law, which is how Travis got a lot of his firsthand information.

Travis was in the Coast Guard from 1951 to 1954. He married Frances Meiggs in 1953. When he got out of the Coast Guard, he attended Campbell College for a year and a half. He came home and started farming in 1956. In 1957, he also started in the long-distance trucking business to haul his own produce. To keep drivers, he had to give them year-round work, and to do this he had to haul produce out

of Florida in the winter. He was soon in the trucking business more than he was farming.

While he had drivers in the trucks, he also guided sportsmen in the winter during the duck hunting season. One winter, he commercial fished. All of this was done to try to make a living and stay in Currituck. He followed these professions until 1970, when he and Frances got their real estate licenses and started Currituck Realty, a business he still owns forty years later.

In 1971, he took people across Currituck Sound in an old gas boat and out to the beach in an old Corvair for which he paid fifty dollars. He'd written "Currituck Realty" on the side of the car with white shoe polish. He sold oceanfront lots for $12,000 that are now valued at over $1 million.

In 1974, he operated Monkey Island Club and opened it to the public for the first time since its founding in 1876. He did this for four years during the process of selling it with three miles of property for the Penn family from Reidsville, North Carolina. They had owned the club since 1932. Charles A Penn was one of the founders of American Tobacco Company.

In 1983, Travis and John H. High started Piney Island Club, which Travis is still a member of.

Frances died in 1992 and Travis married Jo Ann Hayman in 1995.